What People Are Saying about *The Red Book*

"GORGEOUS! *The Red Book* is a deep, smart, and authentic guide to being more indelibly and powerfully yourself."

—SARK, author/artist, *Succulent Wild Woman*

"Beak's vision is a modern, femme fatale spirituality. The book lives up to its 'unorthodox' subtitle, advocating that young women search for the spiritual in all things."

—*Publishers Weekly*

"Every so often there comes our way a glorious chunk of life so utterly unique that even the jaded blink twice. *The Red Book* is just such a chunk, gloriously dropped out of the mind of Sera Beak as a special message for today's contemporary woman in the language of just such a woman, placing before us the wisdom of the ages. From gentle meditation to bouncing sexuality and much in between, the path to personal rejuvenation through the enlivening of the heart, mind, and spirit is laid out in such refreshing, sparkling, effervescent words that what results is a psychic shower for the soul. Get naked, get in, get wet. You'll never feel as clean."

—Neale Donald Walsch, author, *Conversations with God*

"*The Red Book* wrests spirituality from the death grip of the humorless believers and restores it to its wild natural state. If you're hungry for real magic but allergic to self-righteous jive, sit yourself down at this feast."

—Rob Brezsny, syndicated columnist, Free Will Astrology

The Red Book

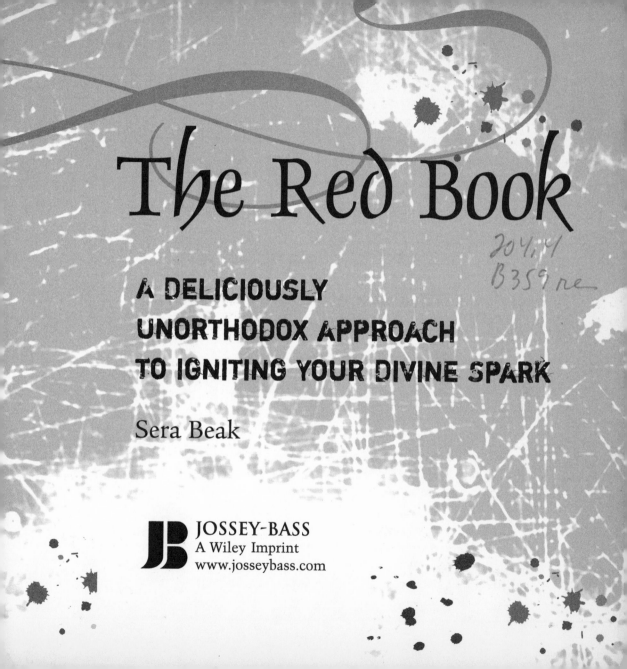

The Red Book

A DELICIOUSLY UNORTHODOX APPROACH TO IGNITING YOUR DIVINE SPARK

Sera Beak

JOSSEY-BASS
A Wiley Imprint
www.josseybass.com

Published by Jossey-Bass
A Wiley Imprint
989 Market Street, San Francisco, CA 94103-1741 www.josseybass.com

Jossey-Bass books and products are available through most bookstores. To contact Jossey-Bass directly call our Customer Care Department within the U.S. at 800-956-7739, outside the U.S. at 317-572-3986, or fax 317-572-4002.

Jossey-Bass also publishes its books in a variety of electronic formats. Some content that appears in print may not be available in electronic books.

Rumi, J., *The Essential Rumi,* (C. Barks with J. Moyne, A. J. Arberry, R. Nicholson, trans.). San Francisco: HarperSanFrancisco, 1995. Used by permission of Coleman Barks.

Tom Robbins, *Esquire,* Oct. 1993. Used by permission of Tom Robbins.

Library of Congress Cataloging-in-Publication Data
Beak, Sera, date.
The red book: a deliciously unorthodox approach to igniting your divine spark / Sera Beak.
    p.   cm.
Includes bibliographical references.
ISBN-13: 978-0-7879-8054-2 (pbk.)
ISBN-10: 0-7879-8054-4 (pbk.)
1. Spiritual life. I. Title.
BL624.B393 2006
204'.4—dc22   2006006224

Printed in the United States of America
FIRST EDITION
PB Printing 10 9 8 7 6 5 4 3 2 1

CONTENTS

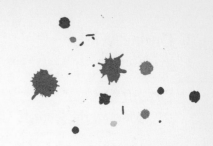

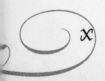

xi

For Grandmother and Grandfather Beak:
A Catholic and a Jew who taught me
that love knows no boundaries, that
exploring this wondrous world is a necessity,
and never to underestimate the
power of a good pun

PREFACE: PRELUDE TO A KISS

Do you ever get that funny feeling, slightly surreal and disorienting, maybe late at night or early in the morning, maybe right before lunchtime or perhaps when your friends are chatting, a lover is changing, a job is droning, or a TV is flickering, a feeling that there's something *more* than all of this? That *you* are more than all of this? That perhaps life is more purposeful and magical than you give it credit for, and never mind all your unpaid parking tickets and bad work days that seem to prove otherwise?

You do? Me, too. As does your best friend, your boss, and your weird neighbor. As do Russian rocket scientists, Belgian sheep farmers, and the Dalai Lama. The feeling is, in fact, universal.

So, what *is* this funny feeling? Sure, you could explain it away as some Freudian childhood glitch or planetary retrograde or even some of last night's margaritas coming up for an encore. But more likely, it's something a bit more profound. Chances are it's a coy catcall from the universe, disguised as existential angst. It's the divine ringing your inner doorbell. It's your higher self, stealing the spotlight. It's your potential, aching to be realized, and your spirit, itching to be scratched. So then the question becomes, what are you going to do about it? Are you going to explore this feeling? Are you willing to open the door? Are you willing to refocus your lens?

If the answer is yes, here's a book that can help. True, it's a book about spirituality, but it's probably not like anything you've read before. It's been created with you and me in mind. Just being real. Just being our true selves. Just being. So let's get started.

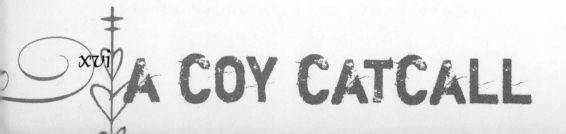

A COY CATCALL

INTRODUCTION: WAKE UP

When sleeping women wake, mountains move.
—CHINESE PROVERB

Are you aware of the rather radical fact that, in truth, not only are you naturally spiritual but you are actually divine? Yes, you, young lady. And you need to start acting like it. Most of us have probably heard some variant of the old "you are divine" cliché. It's a nice, catchy spiritual phrase that gets some people off a bit, a cute little bumper sticker on your soul's VW. Let's keep the mystical meaning but lose the sappy cuteness. Let's undress this most flirtatious of phrases.

Like it or not, if you are alive, then you are spiritual. Let me repeat: If you exist, you can't *not* be spiritual. But you *can* be unaware of this fact, deny it, forget it, take it for granted, hide from it, limit it. It's all too easy, given the general chaos of the world, from religious dogma to political turmoil to relentless fashion trends to ruthless media messages, to feel detached from such an empowering suggestion, to ignore your true makeup, to inhibit your remarkable potential, and to keep your sight dim, your life experience at a low heat, devoid of any yummy sacred sizzle.

Well, enough of that. This book will not let you live that way anymore. *The Red Book* is a candid companion on your spiritual path, an inspirational tool, a winking friend whispering warnings. But more than anything else, it's a fire starter. It will heat up your existence by demonstrating, through ancient wisdom and modern discovery, creative self-expression and hilarious examples, that you are innately spiritual. It also offers clear, powerful exercises so you can begin to experience the fact that you are divine, not just take this book's word for it. After all, you're not merely a human who's struggling to have a spiritual experience. You are, in truth, a spirit, having a human experience. You are not trying to experience divinity so much as divinity is trying to experience *you*. Think about it. Let it soak in for a minute. It is, quite possibly, the most important distinction you can ever make.

At this point, you may be wondering who the hell *I* am to be saying such grand and slightly fluffy things. What right do I have to make such claims? Perhaps I should start at the beginning.

Losing My Religion

I was a weird kid. Besides believing I could talk with inanimate objects (rocks, cars, light switches, apples—you name it, I talked to it) and besides making all my friends and family members refer to me as a different fairy-tale heroine each day of the week (my kindergarten diploma states, "Sarah [Snow White] Beak"), I was slightly obsessed with, well, God. In fact, I desperately wanted to

be a nun, drive a pink Trans Am, and own a parrot—all at the same time. I looked at priests and nuns like other kids looked at sports heroes or movie stars, and even though I was bored out of my mind at mass and Sunday school, I loved the dramatic stories and colorful characters in my children's Bible. Religion was magical and utterly mysterious to me. It hosted miracles and bizarre rituals, angels and demons, saints who levitated and mystics who healed the sick, and fantastical otherworldly places like heaven and hell. For me, at that time, religion offered limitless possibility. It was better than any fairy tale, because it was real (well, sort of).

But then a shift occurred. When I was in sixth grade, I read a book about a psychiatrist who regressed his patients back to their childhood using hypnosis, to help them heal their childhood wounds (yep, I skipped right over Judy Blume in favor of stuff like this). One day, much to his (and his patient's) surprise, the psychiatrist ended up regressing his patient back a bit further than childhood, into what he finally recognized was a *past life*. And in the process, the patient was healed of the ailment she had come to see him about. How odd. He soon began to regress most of his willing patients into their past lives and to places *in between* their lives where they could converse with spirit guides and dead relatives and receive what was often quite profound and healing spiritual information. Whether this doctor was for real concerned me not at all. What intrigued me was the *possibility* that organic spiritual information and wisdom could be available to *anyone,* not just priests or holy people or sketchy corner-store psychics. I liked this. It made me wonder, what if God was still speaking? What if an ordinary (OK, slightly eccentric) Jane like me could receive her own spiritual insights, her own wisdom, her own adventure? Reading about the psychiatrist and his regression technique reminded me that the universe is huge, bigger than I thought, and that I have the freedom to explore it. Not only the freedom, but the responsibility.

Wildly excited about all this new spiritual possibility, I marched straight into confession the following Saturday and immediately started babbling to the priest about reincarnation and spirit guides and other dimensions, thinking he'd be equally excited. He wasn't. He tried very quickly to shut me down. The poor, overwhelmed priest explained that when we die, we simply go to heaven or hell (and he really emphasized the *hell* part), not into other lives. But then I asked him why reincarnation was a big part of Christian belief until the third century (I had found that out after doing a little research), at which the priest got flustered and sent me out of the confessional. I know many priests today who would be more open to this subject, but for some reason, this guy was in the booth that day, and frankly, I'm glad he was. I left the confessional for the last time. I realized, quite suddenly, that Catholicism was not big enough for me anymore.

Walking out of the church that day, I heard an inner applause (in fact, I think I actually bowed), not due to some cocky bravado or because I knew I was leaving Catholicism per se, but because I sensed I was opening myself up to even more wonder, even more divine possibility. I believe you can experience this sort of openness while remaining within a traditional religion, but a huge part of my particular path was about leaving "my father's house" so I could start building my own.

xx

When I went home that day, I informed my wonderfully open-minded Catholic parents that I would not be attending mass anymore. Much to their credit, they (reluctantly) said that was fine but that I must still explore and find out what I *did* believe in. Fair enough. I sometimes wonder whether they ever wish they could retract that directive, because explore I did, and still do, and will, I imagine, for a long time to come. You could say I've taken my explorations pretty seriously. I've studied world religions in intellectually rigorous universities, performed extensive anthropological field research all over this spinning globe, and conducted interviews with several mystics and ordinary religious people.

I've trekked in Tibet and whirled with dervishes in Turkey. I've volunteered at Mother Teresa's Home for the Dying in Calcutta and run from rabid dogs outside Buddhist temples in Kathmandu. I've attended intensive spiritual healing workshops in Sedona and psychic fairs in Chicago, fire rituals in the Black Rock Desert and yoga retreats in Mexico. I've had my past lives read, my aura tuned, my chakras aligned, my spirit guides channeled, my palms interpreted, and my kundalini awakened. I've prayed in churches, temples, mosques, studio apartments, Wiccan festivals, and always, always on rickety buses in India.

I've washed Hindu gurus' feet, eaten dinner with living saints, argued with Zen masters, and had life-altering visions with shamans. I've taught a Tantric Tibetan Buddhist monk how to use his new digital camera, taken the host from a Croatian Catholic mystic who had the stigmata, and had an engaging private audience with His Holiness the Dalai Lama on my twenty-first birthday.

I've studied the Bible, the Koran, the Upanishads, and Buddhist sutras, as well as all the popular spiritual self-help teachers, from Deepak Chopra to Caroline Myss, Marianne Williamson to Andrew Weil, Wayne Dyer to Oriah Mountain Dreamer, and many of the more esoteric alternative authors like Alice Bailey and Edgar Cayce, David Icke and Jane Roberts. I've watched the fads and trends of America's spiritual culture with rapt attention and have talked with countless people my age about their own spiritual experiences, issues, and ideas. Through my years of exploring, I've come to realize that like most people in my generation, I am anti-authoritarian and a little individualistic. I want to find God in my own way, in my own time, and, essentially, by my own self. And I have. She beats deep inside my chest. I see her reflected everywhere. She grows with me.

Yep, I'm a true modern devotee. I love the mystics and *The Matrix,* yoga and the White Stripes, meditation and designer jeans. In terms of cultural dialects, I am multilingual. I speak New Age and Aveda skin care, Eastern philosophy and *Elle* magazine, metaphysics and Hitachi vibrators. I love modern art and dinner parties, lavender chocolate and dirty martinis, dancing and random road trips and hanging out with my girlfriends. My spirituality is real, alive and active, funky and fresh. It's not separate from my daily life; rather, it's so integrated and infused I can no longer separate the two.

So what, you may be wondering after all this, actually is my spirituality? What, exactly, do I believe in? Excellent question; no easy answer.

A Path with Heart

My spirituality is not traditional, although I have learned and continue to learn from the mystical hearts of the world's religious traditions. It is not New Age, although I have learned and continue to learn from many aspects of this dizzying movement. I do not have a guru or one teacher I follow, although I am deeply grateful for the wise teachings of many. I follow my own red heart. I listen to those who speak from their own. And I am wide open, but extremely discerning. I question, doubt, and dare to know there's always more. I sift and dig and only digest the spiritual ideas, tools, and practices that intuitively resonate with me, that challenge me to grow, that allow me to unfold organically. I do not worship these spiritual tools or believe them to be infallible or only touch them with kid gloves. I am deeply respectful, but I also like to rough 'em up a little, tattoo them with my initials, open them up for some fresh air, and fold them into my personal experiences. I get creative with my spirituality. I get physical. I laugh my ass off. I am, as many are, a sort of spiritual cowgirl. And I believe this honest, heart-driven approach has allowed me to have a juicier and more tangible, messy, and free relationship to the divine and to my self (which, as we now know, are ultimately one in the same). As the writer D. H. Lawrence put it, "It is a fine thing to establish one's own religion in one's heart, not to be dependent on tradition and second-hand ideals. Life will seem to you, later, not a lesser, but a greater thing" (p. 256).

My approach is not new. It echoes the experiences and insights of seekers on many different spiritual paths. But my particular

SPIRITUAL COWGIRL

xxiii

expression of this approach is a bit more modern, a bit more female, and, I'm guessing, a bit more like you.

I wrote this book because I didn't find all of myself reflected within the spirituality books I studied over the years. Although packed with wisdom, they were, more often than not, too bland, too serious, too academic, or too woo-woo, and mostly aimed at an older audience. I wrote this book because I know that our culture's lack of youthful, modern feminine perspective is part of the reason why many young women are not strongly drawn to spirituality in the first place. I wrote this book because whenever I ask my friends and colleagues about spirituality, it invariably reminds them of their traditionally religious grandmother or their hemp-covered ex-roommate or a sweaty go-get-'em Jesus-is-your-only-savior TV evangelist, and that's just not gonna cut it. We need some new touchstones, new reference points; *The Red Book* aims to be one.

Truth is, most of us have become pretty jaded when it comes to spirituality and religion, due to some combination of personal history, family, schooling, friends and, of course, all the chaos we see erupting all over this confused spinning planet. On one hand, we see cultures engaging in bloody wars and violence over religious beliefs. We see repression and orthodoxy and conservative Bible-thumping, power-craving agendas. We see the negation of females and their sexuality; we see burqas and genital mutilation; we see fear of the new, fear of the other, fear of God and hell and dildos. On the other hand, we see spiritual traditions like Kabbalah (thanks, Madonna), yoga (again, thanks, Madonna), Buddhism (thanks, Richard Gere and Beastie Boys), meditation, and astrology become ever more mainstream (Gucci incense holders, anyone?)

xxiv

along with the slightly narcissistic New Age and hugely popular self-help movements that want to help us "find ourselves" or "our soulmate" in one weekend for only $599. (Oh yeah, don't get me started on the severe lack of a cool spiritual parlance. Words like *spirit, divine, prayer, soul, universe, God* and phrases like *higher self, inner power, love yourself, find yourself* make some of us cringe, but you'll have to bear with me because it's all we've got for the moment, and as overused and cheesed out as these words may be, they still can, with the right intention and tone, inspire us to reach further and grow stronger.) All of these associations can make the term *spirituality* seem more than a little confusing, a little trendy, a little bloody, a little too touchy-feely.

So what's a smart, gutsy, spiritually curious young woman to do nowadays? Well, how 'bout taking spirituality back into your own hands? How about finding out what it means for *you*, through your own explorations and experiences and expressions? You know, all this spiritual stuff doesn't have to be so esoteric or traditional or weird or dorky or intimidating or holier-than-thou. Spirituality is not separate and distinct from you and your everyday life. Igniting your divine spark is a simple perspective shift. An internal nod. An expanded relaxation into All That Is. It's about tuning up your senses, cranking up your antennae, generating conscious living. It's about becoming your own spiritual authority.

I have no interest in trying to convince you to start creating a more conscious and intimate one-on-one relationship with the universe swirling around you and (more important) the universe flaming bright inside you. But I can speak from my own experience and admit that when I dare to wink back at the divine, when I open

my life to what deliciously includes but also is somewhat beyond
my five senses, life becomes much more flavorful. Profound meaning illuminates even the most mundane of events. My relationships
deepen. My voice becomes clearer. My work excels. My personal
issues become less draining and dramatic. I am less affected.
I require less outside approval. My self-confidence beams. I laugh
more. I judge less. My sexuality roars. Random acts of kindness
become a necessity, not just a whim. (When you start to recognize
your own divine spark, you start to recognize it in everyone and
everything.) My perspectives are amplified. I see the world around
me at much more than face value, and as a result, I make clearer
choices across the board, from my career to my relationships to
my material desires, from politics to the environment to pop culture. I realize I'm not just some well-dressed biped trudging through
life but actually an incredibly powerful and integral piece of the
divine pie. I am In Love. Until, that is, someone cuts me off in traffic.
Then I swear like a sailor and my body tenses and I rain down
Tibetan curses upon their heads. I'm no saint or guru, no absolute
authority. I'm far from perfect at touching tongues with the divine.
But I *have* tasted enough to know that it's the only way I want to
move through this world. Yep, it's that good.

    But.

Know this: Igniting my divine spark has also kicked my ass five ways
from Sunday. My ordinary perceptions are constantly challenged.
My limits are made clear, and then broken open. I cannot play safe
or dumb or keep myself cocooned or judgmental. My unhealthy
patterns, issues, and parts of me that are not in alignment with
my divine spark come up for confrontations all the time. In order

to learn who I really am, I have to learn who I really am *not*. It's not always pretty. It's definitely not always fun. Truth sets me free, but it can sometimes hurt like a thousand bee stings and a bad colonic. I have ended what felt like good relationships, moved across the country, made risky career moves, gotten pretty ill, changed my lifestyle, and experienced extended periods in which I've been lonely as hell and sexually disinterested, all in response to my spiritual path. My sense of self has expanded and contracted like a schizophrenic accordion. I have questioned everything, and I have felt nothing. I have told the universe to fuck off, and I have fallen down weeping at its compassionate response.

But despite the occasional existential tantrums and internal scrubbings, I can still wholeheartedly say that igniting my divine spark is worth it. Learning how to live my truth, out loud and on purpose and with inner authority, is worth it. Merging my humanity with my divinity is worth it. Becoming responsible for my self, for the vibe I give off, feels, well, downright heroic. Just being here, open and ready, is worth all the dirty laundry you can throw at me. And I would rather be alive, be real, be increasingly conscious of all that I am, than move around this planet all mechanical and unconscious.

You know those people you meet whose eyes are sort of vacant and dull, lifeless? Those who are just slumping along life's crowded highways, not ever really reaching deeper into their soul's pockets? What about the opposite type, those whose eyes dance and beam and cry and flash? The ones who seem to glow, despite their imperfections, who tend to attract good friends and good happenings like a magnet, who seem to beam out a calm and fearless sense of self?

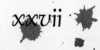

Well, which would you rather be? How clearly do you want to see? I thought so. Here's looking at you, kid.

Let's Lay This Puppy Out

While *The Red Book* can be read cover to cover, it's far from linear. It's written in such a way that it can fall open to what's needed at the time, in a format that allows you to learn what you want, when you want, without having to read the entire book at once. In Chapter One, we set our intention for what will come. Chapters Two and Three are an intellectual warm-up, a sort of clearing of the spiritual throat. They directly address what to be aware of when you are exploring spirituality and religion and ask you to confront any spiritual misinformation you may be dragging around with you, as well as remind you to be respectful of all that you find.

We then move on to more delicious methods of igniting your divine spark, from lipstick prayers scribbled on a bathroom mirror to trusting your intuition when choosing a job, from learning how to read spiritual signposts in everyday life to practicing more mindful meditation. We'll discuss what it means to become more present in the moment, more sexually conscious and more self-aware, along with tips on deciphering your nightly dreams and how to avoid becoming overly attached to those new jeans. We'll go deep and talk about the need to question your fondest beliefs and strip away things in life that inhibit your potential. It's all about paradox, mystery, meditation, sexuality, long walks, and momentous haircuts. It's about becoming more self-expressive and spiritually transgressive

and laughing our way to the end. It's blasphemy made fun, made sacred, made useful.

Of course, these are big topics. Each chapter of this book has the potential to be a full book in itself—and in fact, your local bookstore is full of them. This obviously isn't *Ten Simple Steps to Total Everlasting Bliss*. The ideas covered here are simply entry points. More than anything, *The Red Book*'s objective is to coax new questions out of you, so you can turn around and start actively looking for your own answers. And then you can start sharing them with the rest of us.

I encourage you to avoid letting *The Red Book* be just another cute, barely read addition to your bookshelf or coffee table. Like all the spiritual information available today, this book is absolutely worthless without your full participation, your personal touch, your intention and desire to go further. I've included a colorful resource section, full of some of my favorite books, teachers, Web sites, and other pertinent information to keep you going.

Remember, this book is not so much a general guidebook as my individualized *approach:* a highly selective, somewhat subjective way of perceiving and cultivating one's connection to the divine. I offer this red approach for two simple reasons: First, after all my crazy experience and study, these are the ideas that have stuck, the ones that have worked best for me so far; and second, I believe this approach is reasonably clear, accessible, and an invaluable way for modern young women to initiate a profound yet sloppy bear hug with the universe.

Now, I fully realize (and, in fact, celebrate) that what works for me might not work for you. But I'm confident that many of

the tools and suggestions in this book are universal enough for just about any spiritually energized modern woman to connect with and use to find some wisdom. While you might not find perfect personal resonance on every page (and it would be odd if you did), I can almost guarantee that somewhere in the book, you'll find an opening, a doorway (and hopefully, far more than one) that invites you to pass through in your own unique way. Indeed, the process by which you go about igniting your divine spark will look different from mine and your best friend's and your mom's and that spiritual master's, and that is something to honor. Deeply. We are not here to match and homogenize and agree on every point. One size of spirituality does *not* fit all. We are here to be our divine selves, boldly, passionately, respectfully, to the absolute best of our ability— and this, this is more than enough.

Dare yourself to disturb the universe.

Ask yourself:

How intensely do I want to exist?

xxx DARE YOURSELF

The Red Book

CHAPTER 1

Light the Match
Set Your Intentions Free

So how the hell do you start igniting your divine spark? Well, first and foremost, start by setting your intention. Your intention is the energy, the electric charge, the awareness you bring to every aspect of your life. It's the force that lies behind everything you do, the fuel for your fire. Your intention helps create the pathway for your experience; therefore, setting it ain't no trifling, careless thing, but a *responsibility,* one not to be taken lightly.

Intention is big. Countless are the spiritual books and teachers that discuss, in great detail, just *how* we should set our intentions (check the resource section for just a few that I find helpful). But here in *The Red Book,* I want to keep it simple, by asking you to use intention in a way that helps you give more conscious direction and divine spark to life's ordinary and extraordinary moments.

Setting your intention is a bit like offering up an invocation to the universe. You place your desire out in the world, as an energized thought, a pregnant idea, an open prayer. You envision how you would like to be, to feel, to progress. So let's prime your spiritual engine right now. Begin by stating—and I mean this literally—*how* you would like to interact with this book and how you would like to connect more deeply with the eagerly awaiting universe. Take a deep breath, and slowly let it out. Relax your body, quiet your mind, and let your intention rip, speaking either out loud or internally, or writing boldly in a journal. It might sound something like this:

"This is my intention. I intend to begin igniting my divine spark, consciously. I intend to really know who I AM. I intend to creatively express myself, as authentically as possible. I intend to explore what the divine means to me and what I mean to the divine, to stare straight at the contradiction that claims that the divine is both within me and outside of me, and laugh. I intend to make the red approach my own, to pay attention to my intuition, and to absorb only the spiritual material inside and outside this book that aligns with my divine self. I intend to intend more. I intend to be discerning yet have an open mind and heart and a fantastic sense of humor throughout this whole weird, sticky, delicious process."

Brava! You've rolled the cosmic dice. This is beautiful and good. This is juicy and right. If there's any more or less you'd like to intend now, please do it. And keep doing it. Anytime, anywhere, and about anything—from the sacred to the profane, the glorious to the mundane, and everything in between. Just make sure you use positive phrasing and avoid stating your intentions in the negative; for example, not "please don't let me screw up this new relationship" but rather "I intend to be healthy and loving in this relationship." No matter what the intention, be sure to state it from your heart.

You can state your intentions every morning before you get out of bed; it's like applying an all-day moisturizer for your spirit: "I intend to be divinely aware and connected today, no matter what." You can sing them in the shower: "I intend to follow my gut on this business deal and make it soar." You can let your intention move through your body during a yoga class: "I intend from now on to be healthier with my eating and exercise habits, and to love my

ROLL THE COSMIC DICE

3

strong, sexy body." Or set it when you take a stroll in the park: "I intend to genuinely smile at every thing and every body I come across." You can set an intention for the coming day, week, year, or lifetime, or just for the moment you are in right now. It's really that simple. If you don't have a specific intention to set, just sit still, check in with your heart, and start sensing how you would ideally want to *feel* in your job, in your personal relationships, in your body, in your life, in your relationship with the divine. Hold these feelings strongly for a moment in your mind and heart, and then release them, breathe them out into the world.

This is the divine gist: Setting and holding a clear, strong intention for how you would like your life and your self to unfold, be the intention specific ("I intend to find a great parking space") or universal ("I intend to tread lightly on the planet and make the world a better place"), helps you wring the most divine juice out of every situation, so you become less dependent on the *doing* and more able to enjoy just *being*.

Sound good? Excellent. Now let's talk about the Big G.

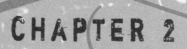

CHAPTER 2

The Beaming You Who

Gods, Goddesses, and the Blind Man's Elephant

*G*od. The word is just so damn loaded. It's endured thousands of years of misuse, and all too often dredges up notions of my God versus your God, or some robed, bearded white male scowling at us from up in the clouds, or some big, approving deity every gushing sports icon or rock star thanks when they win the Super Bowl or a Grammy. Or it brings up that foreboding and vaguely uncomfortable feeling you used to get back in Sunday school or Hebrew school. Or maybe it's a name that caused you to roll your eyes during a philosophy class or a progressive political gathering or a dinner party. For the young and hip, the culturally liberal, or the religiously tired, the concept of God, well, it's rarely thought of as a pleasant thing. But who or what is God?

Rumi, the luminous thirteenth-century Persian mystic and poet, explained humankind's confusion about God by way of a famous story, known as the parable of the blind men and the elephant. It goes like this:

A community of blind men heard that an extraordinary beast called an elephant had been brought into the country. Since they did not know what it looked like, they resolved to find the animal and obtain a "picture" by feeling the beast—the only possibility that was open to them . . .

One man felt the elephant's trunk and declared the creature to be like a water pipe. Another man brushed the elephant's ear and stated that the creature was like a fan. Still another man touched the

6

tusks and found the creature to be sharp. Another man rubbed the leg of the elephant and declared the creature to be like a pillar, while the last man felt the elephant's back and believed the creature to resemble a throne.

This, explained Rumi, is exactly like the various human beliefs about God. All are absolutely convinced they know exactly what it is, yet none can see the big picture and thereby realize that each of their beliefs illuminate part of the same essence, the same overarching energy, the same big honkin' divine pachyderm.

And so it is for you. Explore spirituality for about ten minutes, and you can't help but come face to face with a whole crazy plethora of ideas about the Big G (God). It's a mad mix of possibility that can be at once exciting and daunting, intriguing and incredibly confusing. From uptight, judgmental, fear-based definitions of the divine to sappy, glossy vanilla-pudding incarnations and everything in between, there is no end to what people (and teachers and books and classes and yogis and priests and your massage therapist et al.) can mean when they utter the G word.

The Red Book takes the it's-all-the-elephant view. The divine manifests through all forms (as well as the formless) and therefore has an untold number of faces. In the Hindu faith alone, there are around 300 *million* active deities, not to mention special rocks, mountains, rivers, and other geographical features, all of which are believed to be individualized faces of Brahman, the absolute, limitless, infinite Being or Ultimate Reality. In Hinduism, your *ishta deva* ("divine face," or deity of choice) can be the one you grew up with or the one you are naturally drawn to later on; it doesn't really matter, because in theory (in practice, it may not always be so

⇒ Going Godless ⇐

Several eastern religions and philosophies do not specify any sort of god at all. Buddhism emphasizes the abstract idea of nonbeing, which is more a state or condition than a thing. Taoism embraces the Way, in which all of life is believed to be permeated by the ultimate formless Tao, or Source. The Way of Tao is a flowing, dynamic relationship to this life, created through intense inner concentration and various methods of *wu-wei,* or nonaction. Both of these amazing traditions (which each encompass several sects and schools of thought) highlight the importance of quieting the mind through meditation, staying present, practicing nonattachment, being instead of doing, going with the flow, and accepting where we are right now—all very important ways to help ignite your divine spark and all of which will get much more attention later in this book.

easy), there is no right or wrong deity or spiritual practice because essentially *all* Hindu deities and practices lead back to the same goal: the divine, or Brahman. They are all merely different streams feeding into the same river.

Mystics from every tradition have experienced this kind of Oneness, beyond the pesky details of a strict interpretation. It is a complete taste of the divine that unites rather than separates—and this deliciously profound experience comes from cultivating and

trusting their *inner* experience, not from debating theology and pinpointing external differences. It's an experience of being connected to everyone and everything in the universe to such a degree that peace and nonviolence are the most natural things in the world. (This is exactly the kind of spiritually unifying idea that inspired Gandhi, Martin Luther King, and the current Dalai Lama.)

All of which adds up to this point: When you're exploring spirituality, be aware that authentic divine truth never separates people from each other, countries from each other, religions from each other. There is no right text or correct religion that you must believe, at the expense of all the others. There is no absolutely right God or path or practice. As modern mystic Ron Roth believes, anyone who tries to convince you that there is one right path clearly isn't all that convinced themselves. If a tradition or belief system or teacher expands your definition of the divine, gives it some fresh air, an empowering makeover, a more accessible and body-tingling reality, drink it up. If another's definition of the divine makes you feel like burying your head in a bag of Cheetos or urges you to burn this book in your oven, then spit it out.

In the *Upanishads,* the sacred Hindu texts from the seventh-century B.C.E., the divine is often referred to as *neti neti* (roughly translated, "not this, not this"). This term suggests that divine truth can only be found through the *negation* of all thoughts about it. In effect, the only way to get close to describing the divine is to describe what it's *not.* But the absolute opposite is also true: The only way to describe the divine is to describe everything it *is* (which is, uh, everything). So even though it's nearly impossible to capture

God in words, sometimes it helps, especially at the beginning of a conscious relationship, to find a word or feeling that helps you to focus your experience of the divine. (Brilliant astrologer Rob Brezsny, author of *Pronoia Is the Antidote for Paranoia*, encourages people to create their own name for their experience of the divine. My favorite of his is "The Booming Ha Ha." A couple that I've created are "The Wiggling Wow" and "The Beaming You Who." But let's focus.) For you, the divine could be a specific deity, Buddha nature, the God of Western religion, your higher self. Or the divine could be a bit more abstract and faceless concept, like cosmic energy; something closer to home, like nature or life; more of a feeling, like a deep intuitive tingle or a profound sense of calm; an emotion like love; and so on. Choose any, choose all. Whatever it is, deepen your relationship to it. Get up in its face. Allow it to be an open concept; allow it to be free; allow it, even, to be you.

The Big G, with Breasts

There is one luscious aspect of divinity that deserves a bit (well, OK, a lot) more attention, given how She wears red better than any other and is a huge inspiration for this book. The Goddess. The Divine Feminine. The Big G with Breasts. The one who has, religiously speaking, really gotten the shaft. And this planet's only now beginning to realize that nobody puts Mama in the corner.

For well over two thousand years, patriarchal (that is, male-centric) belief systems have ruled the day. (They still do, but things

10

Be You

are changing faster than you might think.) These dogma-based religions favor control over letting go. They tend to separate rather than unify, monopolize spiritual experience and distrust unique paths that differ from their teachings. Many patriarchal belief systems have taught that this world and our natural human state need to be largely rejected and transcended in order for us to truly know divinity. These belief systems have often found women to be inferior (given their "lowly" connections to the earthly cycles, their unpredictable emotional wiring, and their curvy, tempting bodies) and sexuality to be dirty, a distraction, even a sin. Of course, the biggest oversight in religious history may be patriarchy's failure to acknowledge that despite all our so-called sins, heaven can be found right here on earth; that God moves in love (and meaningful sex), not fear; and that body glitter makes the angels whistle.

Although many of these dogmatic religions have become slightly more receptive to both the divine feminine and women in general in recent centuries, history still leaks into the present, and many modern women have difficulty aligning their sparkly spirits to these male-based traditions. To say the least.

Enter the Goddess. As you probably guessed, most female-centric spiritualities like Wicca (and those that are more earth-centric, like the Native Americans' and those of many other indigenous cultures) tend to be more life-affirming; they value the earth, the body, sexuality, the cycles of nature—in fact, the entire messy, exhilarating, dramatic human experience and all material consciousness—as *positive,* as invaluable, as nothing less than divine.

Sound good? If the Goddess comes knocking on your spirit's door, by all means, invite her in for pie and wine. She might look like the courageous and fierce Egyptian Isis, the astounding Greek athlete and huntress Artemis, or the brainy politician and warrior Athena (also Greek). She could be a sensual lover like Oshun from the Yoruba religion of West Africa, a sacred pipe carrier like the Sioux White Buffalo Woman, a fearless Egyptian warrior like Sekhmet, a promoter of prosperity like the Hindu deity Lakshmi. Goddesses can be sexual gurus, healers, fertility helpmates, intellectual muses, musicians, teachers, dancers, farmers, businesswomen, protective mothers.

Many ancient goddesses (and their modern reinterpretations) emit a salty, sensual flavor. They also tend to be moody and dramatic, delight in collapsing opposites, and can be a unifying powerhouse of divine oomph—an oomph that can't help but add a little glitz to

≈ Mother India ≈

Indian culture, perhaps more than any other, is absolutely *soaked* in goddess worship. Care to hear how the mighty goddess Durga and her bloodthirsty female entourage saved the entire universe from evil demons because the male gods weren't strong enough? Read all about it in the *Devi-Mahatmya*. In Sakta Tantrism (a particularly intense sect of Hinduism), Ultimate Reality is believed to be feminine—not just a mere deity with breasts but the entire universe, worshipped as an abstract Super She!

REDISCOVER

your life while promoting a much-needed attitude change for this planet. And like most faces of divinity, these goddesses could really use a postmodern boost. So invite them into the twenty-first century. Allow them into your life, your bedroom, your workplace. Feel free to rediscover, re-create, and remember. If the old interpretations or forms don't spark your insides, allow a whole new goddess to be remade, through you.

But before we drown ourselves in vulva-worshipping New Ageisms, it must be emphasized that goddess theology is not all rosy-posy. The popular modern belief of many goddess-loving folks—that a strictly female-centered spirituality would answer all the world's problems and give women all the value they deserve (not to mention bigger public restrooms)—well, it's just not entirely true. Just look at India, for but one example, a country with the most active goddess worship today, where millions of women are still undervalued and repressed. We don't need to make the same mistake that many male-oriented religions have made by worshiping in only one direction.

Energy Is More Important Than Form

And now, hear this: Just because you're a young, stylin' modern woman and just because She seems to be the quintessential It Girl these days, that doesn't mean you have to get all go-go Goddess if She just doesn't cut it for you. Hell, you may be sick of deities altogether by this point. The Goddess isn't always easy or ideal. She can be wonderful to explore and connect with and gain insights from, but She's definitely not for everyone.

13

➤ So Why All This ➤ Tra-La-La About Goddesses?

- Because many of us don't even know a divine feminine energy even exists.
- Because even if the particular spiritual beliefs we were raised with assigned no gender to the divine, more than likely, the philosophy and theology encasing them did, and it probably has patriarchy stamped all over it. (Example: A Catholic priest might say to you, "Of course God is genderless," while the whole church chants the "Our Father" in the background.)
- Because, on a red note, many of us don't know that we have the choice to relate to the divine in any way we like and that this is actually much more than a simple gender-colored choice; it is an empowering responsibility that can profoundly change our lives and even the destiny of the planet. So there.

Whoa, drama! How very goddess of me.

What's important for you to cultivate is a connection not necessarily to a particular female icon or ancient deity with shapely hips but to the divine feminine *energy* that ignites them all and, subsequently, all of material and mystical consciousness. In other words, divine feminine energy doesn't necessarily have to take the shape of any particular goddess at all, and it even can be found (if you squint just right) deep within most world religions, not to mention plenty of alternative spiritual traditions, current events, and, more important, your own life. Look around. Start becoming more aware of this universal She-She power that right now is rising up all around you—and inside you.

Sound too vague? Well, it doesn't take a scholar to witness the return of the divine feminine in the twentieth century, from women's political and reproductive rights to environmental movements to *Oprah* to reruns of *Buffy the Vampire Slayer* and *Sex and the City* to a simply astonishing and lovely array of available vibrators; from female priests (though not Catholic, yet) to female senators and CEOs and world leaders and rock stars and athletes and writers. Strong, independent, powerful females and feminine energy are more present and respected than ever before. In fact, Leo Burnett Worldwide, the agency that created the very essence of macho, the Marlboro Man, is having a tough time deciphering the new modern male, largely because, according to Tom Bernadin, the CEO of the company, "The world is drifting toward a more feminine perspective, [and therefore] many of the social constructs men have taken for granted are undergoing significant shifts or being outright dismantled." So there you have it. Culture is changing, on every level. The divine feminine isn't just affecting and re-inspiring women; it's redefining *everyone.*

Now, you might think all this feminine resurgence is just a natural progression of our species, but many current spiritual masters would beg to differ. They believe that there is a necessary shift in overall consciousness going on right now, and that if you're a woman born into this modern age, you have more divine energy available to you than ever before and thus more responsibility to use it wisely. (Don't waste all that energy that courageous women before us have worked so hard for; remember, women only got the right to vote in 1920.) You are being enlisted to fuel a whole new paradigm. You are an integral part of something luminous and new. And what's more, the universe *needs* you to recognize your role and manifest this enlightened feminine energy directly. Do it through your career, relationships, community, politics, beliefs, votes, orgasms, and, most especially, by owning and uniquely expressing your full power. Sound exhilarating? We're only just beginning. This world ain't seen nothing yet!

Who's Your Daddy (or Mommy)?

The Red Book doesn't care what or who represents the divine to you, but it does care very much about *how* your view of the divine affects your inner and outer life. Does your view of the divine allow you to explore and be creative and remain open to diverse people and beliefs? Does it give you inner strength and peace and promote love and deep belly laughs and the desire to help others? Or does your view of the divine make you feel fearful, guilty, small, narcissistic, or overly critical? You'd be surprised at how other traditions or trendy movements—basically, others' Gods—have influenced or even created your ideas, sometimes to the point of blocking your own personal experience and preventing you from exploring further.

Maybe you choose not to believe in any sort of God or divine force whatsoever, and that's just fine. But then, what God are you not believing in? A Judeo-Christian God? A New Age God?

A Buddhist nothing? Your mother's God? (Some of the most color-ful ideas of what God is or isn't come from my atheist friends.) What if you just respectfully kissed all those external notions of divinity good-bye and set out to find out who *you* really are, and by doing this, lo and behold, you found out who God has *always* been? In other words, what if you decided to know God *from the inside out*? What would She (or He) look like? What would She feel like? Who would She actually be?

What if you saw God or the divine as nothing more than you, living your life with all you've got? What happens to you, down at the cellular level, in your very core, where the meanings are, when you experience deep love for someone or something? What's the feeling you get when you look up at the stars or into a newborn's eyes or when you see a dog romping freely and joyfully in the park or when you are enjoying a hysterically funny dinner with friends or running freely, muscles pumping, down a sandy beach, or just sitting silently alone in the woods, awake and aware? What is the sense you have about death? About art? About nature? About claw-foot bathtubs? Keep asking new questions, and keep listening for new answers. You might be surprised at how God or the divine comes through.

It's vitally important to nix any old-school ideas of the divine that weigh you down, squash your inner knowing, dampen your desire to ignite your inner flame. Let the divine reveal itself to you, opening yourself up to it in your own way, in your own time, through any means. Let yourself get creative in your expression. And please don't let the divine be just a mental construct. After all, divinity is experiential, not intellectual. You feel it, you sense it, you

17

intuit it, far more than you need to think about it and analyze it. Don't box it up. Don't plague it with set beliefs. Be willing to create a brand-new relationship.

And even if you feel totally clueless about what/who/where/ why divinity is, it doesn't change the fact that *something's* still there, twinkling your world, illuminating meanings, urging you this way and that, winking and whispering and just waiting to contradict, to surprise, to undress. All you have to do is get quiet inside, hear that whisper, resonate with that sunset, and allow yourself to realize, *Aha,* Here I Am. Here We Are. Now let's get this party started.

CHAPTER 3

Are You Really Gonna Eat That?
Grazing at the Spiritual Buffet, Respectfully

I f you come across a manifestation of divine energy that catches
your heart while you're exploring your divine path, don't keep it
out in the cold just because you're not sure of its background.
Invite it into your life. Offer it a place setting. Get to know it better.
For example, let's say the elephant-headed Hindu god of good for-
tune, Ganesha, catches your spirit's eye. Some quick research might
tell you that he is most often placed near doorways and that his big
belly loves sweets. So, as you get to know him more deeply, perhaps
you put a small Ganesha icon on your hall table and stick a Tootsie
Roll on his lap. You might ask him, with full intent and sincerity,
to only bring good people and good luck to your home. You might
ask him to help you curb your own sweet tooth or to help inspire
you to come home to your true self, or maybe you just nod your
respects and smile at his obvious joy when you open your front
door after a hard day's work.

Perhaps Zen Buddhism is beckoning your spirit? You're not
alone. The simple, beautiful Zen sect of Buddhism is incredibly
popular right now. The simplicity of Zen living might inspire you
to finally clear all the clutter out of your living room, buy a *zazen*
cushion (a square pad used for sitting on the floor) for meditation,
or sign up for a local Zen retreat. You might simplify your diet and
start practicing mindfulness when you visit with your grandmother
or when you make those important phone calls. You might begin to

be able to sit still long enough to hear your inner guidance, even when in the midst of a family reunion or during a concert or on the bus.

Maybe you're drawn to Native American spirituality? Beautiful. Let's say that, as you poke around, you find you resonate with one of the Native Americans' most powerful and sacred totem animals, the eagle. So maybe cut out that picture you love of an eagle in flight from *National Geographic* and stick it on your refrigerator. You might start collecting feathers. You might begin to be drawn to other symbols, music, art, beliefs, and stories that communicate the powers of flight and far-reaching, eagle-like vision. You might use this animal's traditionally worshipped powers of intense clarity to help you avoid getting stuck in a fight about the details of your best friend's wedding or in petty squabbles with your coworker. You might begin to react differently when you hear about a terrorist act or a neighborhood dispute on the news as you begin to see above the fear and politics and meaningless arguing, and seek a broader perspective, a higher method of reasoning—the eagle's view.

You get the idea. Exploring a new spiritual path doesn't have to be complicated. It doesn't have to be ornate or expensive or a big production in your life, a switch away from everything you do and all your regular habits and routines toward some strict new set of habits and beliefs. New spiritual tastes are things you simply start to include in your life, become more aware and appreciative of. Just *fold them in,* like rich chocolate swirls in your divine batter. This is how it begins.

Gorging at the Spiritual Buffet

One thing I hear *a lot* as a result of my spiritual cowgirl status—and this is something you might hear, too, as you progress down your own individual path—is the ol' "spiritual buffet" indictment almost anyone who follows a single tradition or teacher likes to throw my way. The spiritual buffet indictment speaks to the fact that far too many spiritually curious people in this day and age think it's perfectly fine to nonchalantly pick and choose what they want from the tantalizing array of religions and beliefs, books and teachers available in the modern world, only taking what they like, what feels good or looks good or matches their lives the way a nice paint- ing matches their couch, while possibly missing what they might actually *need*: "Om, I'll have the small shamanic salad with lite Vishnu dressing, a side order of Zen, and a fat-free Torah shake with a channeled Star Being sprinkled on top." The assumption or concern is that these spiritual grazers don't really grow; they merely remain on the shallow surface of divine possibility, allowing their ego and personal issues and even unconscious negative habits to determine their spiritual meals. They eat the sweet and easy parts of spirituality ("Yum, goddess twirling is yay fun! Look how cool and spiritual I am!"), but they don't get their necessary spiritual roughage ("Oh shit, this practice has made me realize *I'm* the only reason why my life sucks right now"). They pass over the stuff that's gonna truly fortify them, because it doesn't taste as good and usually requires a bit of work, time, and discipline. Without any clear-cut guidelines, like those from a strict teacher or a tradi-

tion, these buffet addicts merely become more self-involved. They *think* they're being all spiritual, while in fact, they're just breeding more unhealthy patterns.

It all comes down to a simple, but absolutely essential reminder: As you explore, be exceptionally careful not to use spirituality as a cocktail, as just a quick high or a mere inebriating distraction. The point is to use various spiritual practices, beliefs, teachers, and even deities as self-empowering refreshers, to help you sober up for a more authentic divine connection.

The Red Book is not about telling you what you should or shouldn't digest from the spiritual buffet (after all, one woman's meat is another woman's poison), but it does ask you to educate yourself, to be aware that this careless grazing is an easy habit to fall into, and to start paying sufficient attention to your life and your self so that you'll spark your natural ability to know, to sense when you're not getting enough healthy spiritual sustenance. (By the way, we'll explore how to kick-start your intuition to do just that in Chapter Thirteen.) I know, I'm beating this food metaphor to death, but bear with me. Because personally, I've found that if I'm eating too many spiritual sweets, I'll start to feel exactly the way I feel when I'm eating too much *real* candy. A little sticky, a little gross, kind of nauseous, definitely not well nourished or satisfied. And if I ignore this feeling and continue grazing, I'll get a nasty stomachache (literally), eventually bad enough that I'll clue in, take a step back, and start balancing my spiritual diet out so that I can resume spiritual health. Practice makes perfect. Examples? You've got 'em.

SUSTENANCE

23

Chocolate Chip Cookies and Broccoli

When I was in grad school, I was invited to join a wonderful women's circle that was all about celebrating the divine feminine. Smart women, good discussion, tasty snacks. What could possibly go wrong? My heart definitely got excited to beat in that space, but after a few weeks of goddess dancing and repetitive discussions about how special the Goddess is and thus how special we were, I began to feel sort of "false-full." Great intention, nice women, excellent chocolate chip cookies, and nice, whirly rituals that made me feel all sassy and sacred, but I'd leave a meeting and my giddy high would vanish almost immediately. I was left with very little real meat to sustain my everyday reality. Eventually, I even began to feel physically exhausted after the meetings. So, trusting my senses over the feel-good intentions of those terrific women, I left. I realized that getting myself fluffed up like a goddess while eating too many chocolate chip cookies wasn't really helping me feel a deeper, more authentic connection to the divine, nor was it much of a galvanizing force to move me toward a greater understanding of my not-so-simple, not-always-goddessy self.

The truth is, some of the most pleasant, feel-good spiritual material I've come across has eventually left me wistful, drained, and a little lost. It stopped fueling my inner tank. Don't get me wrong, sometimes a little inspiring fluff is just what the spiritual doctor ordered, but when we only allow perky spiritual high fives into our world, we often prevent ourselves from taking much-needed steps toward authentic spiritual growth. And growth is what it's all about.

On the other hand, some of the most profound, life-changing material I've come across has, at first, made me awfully uncomfortable. I once attended a class that taught one essential metaphysical maxim: We, as individual spiritual beings, are solely responsible for much of how our life plays out, because our thoughts and beliefs create our reality. In other words, it's not my experiences in the world that define me but, rather, my *thoughts* about my experiences that create and define the experience.

Uh, what?

Every experience can be interpreted in any number of ways. For example, if someone cuts me off in traffic, I can see it as infuriatingly rude and annoying and let it put me in a nasty mood for the whole day. Or I can choose to perceive the experience differently, maybe seeing that road-raged person as just having a bad day and clearly deprived of good sex. I step back from the whole scene, observe it from a distance, and don't really let it touch me. It's my choice. This is one of the most difficult lessons of all: realizing that when it comes down to it, you can't really blame anybody or anything outside of yourself for ruining your day, your year, your life. Not "evil" terrorists or dysfunctional families or the nasty she-bully from seventh grade, not lousy bosses or a broken heart or really bad hair. The bottom line: I may not be able to control my life, but I can choose how I want to act in *response* to it, and it's these reactions that create and determine my experience. The responsibility is mine, and no one else's.

Now, this idea didn't exactly make me feel great or special or like a hot, sassy goddess. In fact, at first, the idea wigged me out, shook up my safe little world, even scared me (the authentic spiritual path often does) by placing all that spiritual responsibility directly on my shoulders. It was a challenging notion that actually de-numbed me, stripped away my normal excuses and intellectual defenses, which is *never* a comfy feeling. Nevertheless, the class still resonated with my internal gauge; something about it just felt right and empowering, like something that could really help me become clearer about my life and my divine role within it. I knew it wouldn't be easy. I knew the practices and teachings offered through this class would peel my misperceptions back in difficult and even embarrassing ways. But I also knew, deep down, that I had to do it. It was what my spirit wanted. Check that: It was what my spirit *needed*. I stuck around and worked hard and learned how to be more conscious of my thoughts and beliefs, something I practice in a variety of ways (like meditation) to this very day.

It's just another spiritual contradiction: Sometimes what makes you lick your lips with easy excitement might not actually be the best thing right now, whereas what challenges you or frightens you a little or even ticks you off the most is what your spirit *needs* the most. Unconscious fears, subconscious desires, childhood experiences, personality quirks, past lives, ego, what we had for lunch today—the list of forces that manipulate our spiritual choices is long and messy and requires a lot of parsing on your part. And by the way, just as there are lots of people who are only eating spiritual doughnuts, there are also those who will *only* eat raw brown rice that's still rooted in the dirt, and only with a toothpick they whittled from a blessed tree in a blessed Hindu forest under a full moon in Pisces. And guess what? That's not very balanced, either. So what to do? How do you keep yourself in check, while enjoying the magnificent buffet before you?

Follow Your Heart, Not Your Ego

First, set your intention, like we did at the beginning of this book, to be conscious while you're exploring spirituality. Ask the universe to show you some signs if you've strayed way off into la la land or unhealthy territories. (There's lots more on divine signs in Chapter Six.) And ask yourself some basic questions about the spiritual directions you're interested in: Is this book, practice, class, or teacher a healthy addition to my spiritual life? Am I being challenged to be a more attuned person in *all* areas of my life, not just the so-called spiritual areas? Am I encouraged to not just focus on my own self but help others as well (for example, through volunteering, community service, or just being kinder to my loved ones and the neighbor's dog)? Am I encouraged to question beliefs and traditions—even theirs? Am I supported but not coddled in my process? (Hey, we all need the occasional spiritual spanking.) Am I made aware of the dark as well as the light? Am I encouraged to be honest about my issues and to take healthy action? Or am I avoiding some spiritual practice that would help me grow stronger because I know it would be demanding and would upset my easy life? Is compassion toward myself and others a fundamental principle? Am I surrounded by wisdom, nonjudgment, sound ethics, and good humor? You get the idea. When in doubt about working with a certain spiritual practice, I often think about what author and shaman Carlos Castaneda so famously said in his book *The Teachings of Don Juan*: "Any path is only a path, and there is no affront, to oneself or to others, in dropping it if that is what your heart tells you. . . . Look at every path closely and deliberately. Try it as many times as you think necessary. Then ask yourself, and yourself alone, one question. . . . Does this path have a heart? If it does, the path is good; if it doesn't it is of no use" (p. 82).

This is a book about creative spirituality, so it celebrates the fact that we get to mix our own spiritual batter. One meditation practice might be more effective at training you to stay in the present moment and hear your inner wisdom, while the fantastically dry sense of humor of a teacher from a completely different tradition might point out aspects of your self that need serious work. Past-life regressions with an energy healer might help you heal your dark and shine your light, while walking alone on the beach helps you realize you are one with everything, and so on. Our spirits often draw sustenance from several wells, but you should still make sure the overall effect is wholly supportive and authentic. Bottom line: Excess diversity is not always healthy, but neither is *insufficient* diversity. In fact, both can be serious obstacles, just more ways for us to escape sitting down and really looking at ourselves and creating a clearer connection to the divine. It is, as always, all about balance. Remember to actually *walk* the spiritual path of your life; don't spend too much time lingering in the gift shop.

There's Something About Mary

Let's take all this spiritual exploration a step further. Not only do you have every right to respectfully explore all spiritualities and adore any reflection of the divine that resonates powerfully with

28

☞ Take the High Way ☜

Here's the golden rule of exploring: If a tradition or class or teacher is not open to your unique relationship with the divine, asks more from you than you sense it should, tries to force you to do anything that makes you seriously uncomfortable in the name of "divinity," or claims to know the one and only true path to divinity, leave. Quickly. If a teacher or tradition or class says it's their way or the highway, take the High Way. I guarantee you'll ignite your divine spark much faster.

your spirit, but you also have every right to see an aspect or have an experience that is very different than the tradition from which it originates.

Once again: Uh, what?

Let's say that as part of your divine explorations, you choose to dive deep into Buddhism. Chances are that you'll experience a completely different kind of Buddha energy than a person living in Tibet would, because (obviously) you two come from very different cultural and spiritual backgrounds. Your grandfather might experience a very impersonal, harsh, judgmental God due to his regimented military past and strict upbringing, whereas you might experience a very personal, humorous, and nonjudgmental God (or Goddess) due to your laid-back, peaceful background and progressive personal beliefs. Furthermore, your experience of that God or Buddha will (and actually, *should*) grow and change as you grow and change.

29

Here's a powerful example: Let's suppose you were raised with the traditional Christian story of the Virgin Mary. You learned that she was, literally, an immaculate virgin of perfection when she miraculously became pregnant and gave birth to Jesus. Maybe you've been told this story your whole life and never questioned it. This story, then, will heavily influence the teaching, the face, the energy, you will experience when you reflect on Mary. You might respect how intense it must have been to be told, at around fourteen years old, that she was pregnant with God's child and the difficulty of explaining that one to her fiancé and family, but maybe this Mary—traditionally depicted as rather subservient and chaste and not the slightest bit multifaceted or emotionally charged or truly womanly, and often sexually sterilized by the Church—maybe this version of Mary is, well, a little weak and inadequate for you.

But still, it's Mary. She is one powerful icon of religious myth, one of the few women in the Bible with some clout. So let's say there's something about Mary that still resonates within you, and once you strike out on your own spiritual path, you do a bit of research and you learn, via a class, teacher, book, meditation, or your own late-night dream revelation, that the word *virgin*, according to many Greek translations and interpretations, actually means "one unto herself." Hmm. This changes things. This widens meanings. You start thinking about what that might connote, exactly. You realize that maybe those old patriarchal church translations of ancient Greek stories (that is, the Bible) might not, let's just say, have Mary's best interest at heart. Your awareness heats up, shifts, grows a bit wider. A little spicy sauce is added to your perception of the Virgin.

One Unto Herself

So you research more and meditate on this a little further, and lo and behold, you learn that there's a whole panoply of virgin birth myths, spanning a whole range of fascinating religious traditions, most of which predate Christianity, and that the Christian Mary is actually derived from a universal feminine figure that encompasses several ancient goddesses and that's translatable to a multitude of faiths and perspectives. You begin to see Mary not at all as some sterile, sexless vehicle but as a symbol, a potent female *energy force,* stronger, more empowered, more multidimensional, and much more relatable than you'd ever imagined. What's more, maybe you realize that, according to this new, personal definition of *virgin,* you yourself are not quite "one unto herself" just yet, and so you begin to ask this new Mary energy to help teach you how to be more whole and self-empowered. And maybe these new virgin-infused perspectives help you see just how many more steps you need to take in your own life before you, say, walk down that aisle and fully commit to loving someone else. Or maybe it's simpler than that, and your new Mary vibe simply helps you stand up for yourself more often at work. Or stop being so shy. Or choose your lovers more selectively. Perhaps this new, raw Mary vibe of yours will help you become less needy of constant outside affirmation of how you look, how you are liked, or how you perform. And on it goes.

And just like that, your shift of perspective has actually changed the face of Mary for you, and therefore, how you experience her sacred energy will change as well. It is an active, kaleidoscopic relationship. With all due respect to strict religions, these ancient figures and the energies they represent were not meant to be flat and unyielding.

The Outsiders

When I first encountered the fierce Hindu goddess Kali by way of
a vibrant poster that one of my professors had pinned up on the
blackboard, I was immediately hit by a sort of kinesthetic whap. I
had no idea what or who she was, but I did know she made my heart
beat faster and my palms sweat and something deep in me flutter
and pay attention, so I decided to check her out. I took a class
on Indian goddesses, read some books, and eventually even lived in
India for a while, and for my birthday that year was given one of the
fiercest-looking goddess icons I'd ever seen. For a while, my *ishta deva*
(my personal deity or divine face of choice) was this intense Indian
warrior-goddess, a four-armed, sword-wielding, completely naked
(well, except for a skirt made of human limbs and a necklace of
human skulls) female deity who actually predates Hinduism. Kali's
blood-soaked tongue sticks out *at us* (as my favorite transgressive
professor Jeffrey Kripal would say); she has wild hair, likes to be on
top, and, if she so chooses, can dance the universe to death. Unlike
most Hindu deities, she is not married, she traditionally likes to be
worshipped in cremation grounds, and she pretty much scares the
bejesus out of neoconservative Texans and those who are not willing
to face all of themselves in order to become enlightened. But for
those who worship her, she appears beautiful and loving. (In this
case, beauty really *is* in the eye of the beholder.)

To worship Kali—or maybe a better way of saying it is, to
embrace Kali mojo in your life—is to tap into a swift transformative
energy that's all about cutting through illusions—like all your

⪦ God Said What? ⪧

If you find yourself drawn to one of the world's big religious traditions but don't necessarily want to accept all the common ideology surrounding it, I highly recommend delving into the true roots of its sacred texts and prayers. You will often find that the original intention of the text is different from what you might have been taught. For example, "Our Father, who art in heaven," when translated directly from ancient Aramaic (the language Jesus spoke) to English, becomes, simply and beautifully, "O Thou (or O Birther), from whom the breath of life comes." This most famous of Christian prayers then continues in cosmically centered language that's free of gender associations and strict dogma.

The message: Always dig deeper.

Fact is, much of what we know today as traditional prayer or scripture or sutra has been translated from ancient texts (and oral traditions) and filtered through a variety of languages by a handful of very dead men who had their own spiritual beliefs, political or cultural agendas, and, of course, power issues. Religious history is far more subjective than we realize and, like political history, is mostly written by the "winners" (that is, those who conquered the preceding culture). Remember, religion is a manmade invention. Spirit is not. So relax your linear focus a bit. Spirit is winking like mad between the lines. All the lines.

personal issues and fears and domineering ego—so the *real* you (divine self) can come out to play. Although I didn't follow traditional Hindu worship practices, my relationship with Kali was no less acute. Meditating on Kali and being intentionally aware of her wild energy as I remained a modern American gal and went about my daily grad school business was not always easy. Obviously, she ain't your typical soft-focus, pink 'n' fluffy goddess type. No matter my stress level or relationship status, Kali kept me slicing away at unhealthy qualities, from shyness and lack of confidence (in the classroom and the bedroom) to fear of change (and elevators) to unhealthy eating habits and a whole host of other personal crap I consciously or unconsciously clung to. I also learned how to be more actively engaged in *all* the cycles of life—not just the light, feel-good parts but also the dark and confusing and Oh-my-God-I-hate-my-life times— and to view death (including my beloved grandfather's) not so much as a harsh end but as a new spiritual beginning— all teaching specialties of this dark goddess. To this day, she encourages me to write—to *live*—fiercely and from the heart. (There she is, right now, sticking out her tongue at this very sentence as I write it.) Kali is just one of the many divine faces I've rubbed noses with over the years, one that's helped me become more entirely me, not to mention a superstar on any dance floor. And by the way, the color most attributed to Kali? You got it: red.

Miz Appropriation

But now, another snag. See, many traditionalists and politically correct types believe that such divine face-lifting is very disrespectful.

They argue that it's just horribly inappropriate to take part (or even all) of a religious practice, belief, or deity from a well-established religious tradition (as I did with Kali) and use it for one's own selfish, pseudospiritual, or psychotherapeutic needs. I've heard it all: It's theft. It's misappropriation. It's imperialistic and neocolonialist. It's Western-centric, white woman–centric, horribly individualistic, highly egotistical, abusive, and, along with a host of other negatives, just plain wrong.

Ironically, I used to strongly agree, at least intellectually, with parts of these arguments. I knew that these perspectives, although somewhat uptight, provided the belief systems in question with an important theological weight in the West, especially in regard to their effort to control the rampant shallow consumerism that is often applied even to things spiritual throughout American culture.

But what do you do when the spirit becomes stronger than the rational brain? When divinity ignores what is "proper" or "culturally appropriate" and just shows up in whatever crazy form you need most? This is what happened to me. Here I was, plodding my way through grad school, intellectually tsk-tsking those who "misappropriated" spiritualities, but then I'd close my eyes at night and get my head chopped off by Kali in a crazy dream. Or if I wasn't dreaming of goddesses from across the globe, I was coming to some other humble realization, like how a particularly potent Native American totem, the eagle, was, at that particular time, for some mysterious reason, the most effective symbol for inspiring me to communicate more honestly. So of course, I placed a small Native American icon of an eagle on a makeshift altar in my living room. In some ways, I was doing exactly what I frowned upon in those lectures. I was

35

⇒ My Divinity Matches My Shoes ⇒

No question, there are some well-founded reasons to be worried about the West's infamous ability to misappropriate sacred ideas. Just look around: There are too many people with the Sanskrit "om" symbol tattooed on their sacrum or wearing $20 red Kabbalah strings around their wrist (Madonna and Britney wear 'em, so why can't I?) and passing out in sweat lodges without really having a clue as to what these things actually mean or where they come from.

But what about you? How do you know if you're being spiritually materialistic? Again, be responsible. Be respectful. Don't treat spirituality like a cute accessory. Take the time to figure out what the symbols and practices actually *mean*. Do some research, and show them their proper reverence. As Gandhi said, "If we are to respect others' religions as we would have them respect our own, a friendly study of the world's religions is a sacred duty." Ask yourself, How do these spiritual props support me on my path? Why am I *really* using them? Am I being conscious, or have I been reading too much *Us Weekly*? And if you know you're well-informed and are being properly respectful, then, well, I say go for it. Remember, spiritual crossovers happen all the time as the divine continues to squeeze through the narrow eye of human experience. So who's to say the divine doesn't love to be wrapped around your body in a cotton T-shirt or permanently etched onto your sacred sacrum? Not me, that's for sure.

misappropriating like crazy. Should I have shut off all this divine twinkle? I sure as hell tried to, at first. But deep down, I knew I was missing out on what these energies were trying to teach me. I finally learned, despite my initial resistance, the importance of not limiting how the divine shows up in my life and, perhaps most important, not judging how it shows up for others. As French writer and humanist André Gide said, "Believe those who are seeking the truth. Doubt those who find it."

Let Divinity Disco

You'd be amazed at how many traditions absolutely *insist* that certain aspects of the divine are absolutely rigid and inflexible, and if you try to change or adapt them in the slightest, you're not merely dishonoring a major sacred aspect of spiritual life but actually blaspheming, an act punishable by a very unpleasant, fiery afterlife. To which *The Red Book* says, oh please. You've gotta be open to the possibility that the divine is a dynamic, *moving energy*. Throughout time, religions have flowed in and out of one another, causing both subtle and dramatic changes in each culture they have run through and brushed up against. Check these out:

• *Christmas.* In ancient Babylon, the twenty-fifth of December was known as Yule Day, or "the birth of the promised child" day. *Yule,* according to some interpretations, is the Chaldean (a language of Babylon) word for *infant.* This was the day that the sun god Tammuz, one of the biggest deities of 'em all, incarnated as a little baby in order to save the world from darkness. Sound familiar?

• *Easter.* Easter is believed by some scholars to be named after Eostre, a Great Mother goddess of the Saxon people of Northern Europe. Or maybe it was originally a celebration of Cybele, the Phrygian mother goddess who originated in Asia Minor around the fifth century B.C.E. but then made her way all the way to Rome, where they built great temples to her and called her "Magna Mater" (Great Mother). Her son, Attis, died and was resurrected three days later (ahem), a fact that was celebrated each year in late March or early April. Fact is, plenty of pre-Christian cultures in Western Europe observed a holiday during the spring equinox. This festive holiday often celebrated the union of the young Goddess and God, which was believed to help fertilize the community and fields. And what were the symbols employed to represent fertility and abundance? You guessed it: rabbits and eggs.

• *Genesis in the Hebrew Bible.* Check out the ancient Babylonian myth *Enuma Elish,* the Epic of Creation (there are several English translations available), and compare it with the famed Genesis tale ("In the beginning . . .") from the Bible. Not only are the stories eerily similar, but you can still find evidence of *Enuma Elish* in the Torah; God refers to himself as "we," and the goddess Tiamat, the god Marduk, and other deities are alluded to as they duke it out in order to create first light, then water, earth, animals, plants, and good old human beings. All from darkness. *Now* let there be light!

These examples are merely the tip of the research iceberg. There are thousands of examples of this kind of spiritual evolution and sacred plagiarism. Once you start learning about the true history of various religions and spiritual traditions, you can't help but release uptight notions about religious purity and about there being only one true expression of divinity. So celebrate America's famed freedom of religion. Loosen up the bonds of perception. Free yourself from spiritual stagnation. The divine obviously loves to dance, so turn up your spiritual iPod. Be true to the music that comes through you. Honor what prayer wants to create out of you. And be sure to blow Mary and Kali some kisses along the way; after all, they have a lot more in common than you might think.

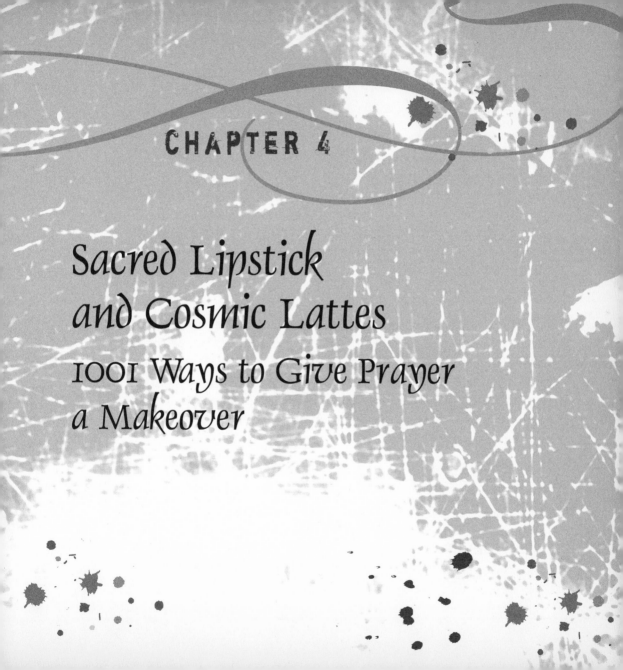

CHAPTER 4

Sacred Lipstick and Cosmic Lattes

1001 Ways to Give Prayer a Makeover

*P*rayer—yet another intensely loaded spiritual word that for many of us has lost the personal connection, the palpable zing, and the broad range of application we are seeking in today's world. Well, it's time to change this, to shake off any repressive or antiquated beliefs about prayer and bring this powerful practice straight into your life, raw and meaningful and new. Even if you're happy in practicing traditional modes of prayer or you never pray at all (except maybe for that perfect parking space), *The Red Book* suggests adding a little something extra to your divine repertoire.

What if you tried a stripped-down, Brazilian bikini-waxed, reclaimed, retuned, redecorated, re-energized experience of prayer? Prayer that originates from your seemingly ordinary life and personality: your relationships, career, joys, frustrations, issues, pop culture, travels, journal, spiritual practices, and, most important, your divine spark? What if you spread open your experience of prayer so wide that you allow your entire life and your entire self to become living, breathing creative prayers?

Booking Red

I try to do just that. All the time. In fact, the title for this very book originated from my own red book, the place where I used to inscribe my own intensely personal creative "prayers." The book it-self was an oversized blank journal, loosely bound in deep, suede-like red cloth, given to me by my wise older sister for my twenty-sixth birthday, just days after we had witnessed my grandfather's death, an event that left us both emotionally raw. Truthfully, I used to detest gifts that asked me to "be creative," perhaps because they brought back uncomfortable memories of flunking my grade-school art classes and because I often felt intimidated, silly, and a little too Martha Stewart–ish trying to do something crafty when I didn't have the natural chops. But my grandfather's death and my weakened emotional state quieted those fear-based voices. And so, late one night about a week after my birthday, I turned off the TV, cranked up a Perfume Tree CD, opened the blank red book, and started writing short, simple phrases. Just to see what would happen. The first page filled with a tearful good-bye and heartbroken thank-you to my beloved grandfather. The next page started with "My body is a map to my soul. Temple me, to find Me"; the next page, "The Closer you are to your Self, the more of You there is to Be"; and I went on from there. The phrases were pretty weird, dramatic, and young, sometimes sensual and provocative, sometimes thick with obtuse poetic fluff, but it was their release, my release, that felt incredibly exhilarating.

I quickly noticed that my short little phrases took up hardly any space on the big, blank 11 x 15 pages, so I decided to use the only other sliceable artistic medium available in my apartment: fashion magazines. Their images, rearranged in capricious collages, turned my simple phrases into meaty spiritual realism, and my honest words gave the advertisements and fashion shoots flashes of sacredness. Soon postcards and art calendars fell into the creative mix, as did various pamphlets I would find pinned to Harvard's

43

bulletin boards: party invites, mascara ads, lecture handouts, yoga images. The real world I inhabited on a daily basis became the medium for divine expression. Over time, as I delved, wrote, cut, and pasted, I began to realize that this practice of writing and collage work was more then just a therapeutic, self-indulgent exercise.

Now, at this point you might be saying, "Oh please, it's just a freakin' journal, everyone has one." But no. This was a brand spanking new experience for me. To be honest, I can't believe the uninhibited power of the voice that started pouring out of me, especially when contrasted with the shy and quiet voice that was my normal mode of communication. When I chose to take a time-out from my busy daily schedule, focused my intention, and gave my expressions free reign, it was like a massive release valve, a deep, profound sigh. *Finally,* said my spirit.

This voice was my divine spark, getting frisky. For the first time in twenty-six years, I was listening, allowing her to speak out loud, and I guess she had a lot to say. As the process evolved and as the conversation between us deepened, I realized that I was, in my own way—and probably for the first time—really *praying.* My creations (prayerlets? prayerecitos?) were messy and raw—my personal dimensions unfolding roughly across a page. This was no kneeling in a church, hands folded carefully together, humbling yourself before some judgmental deity. It was no passive, compliant act of detached piety. It was just me expressing all of my self, privately, nontraditionally, and honestly.

Does this free-form mode of praying creatively sound intriguing? I hope so. One powerful way to learn from this book is to try creating your *own* red book. (Of course, yours might be purple or turquoise, rainbow-colored or gold-glittered). With the right intention, this kind of passionate journaling could give your unique spirit the space it needs to shimmy and help stimulate a deeper knowledge of self. It could ignite your desire to be more creative and self-expressive *outside* the book. Maybe it will remind you that the ethereal dances deep within the tangible. Hopefully, it will make you laugh more and will freak out your best friend just a little. All of these are good and necessary things. The point is to engage the universe in your own funky and meaningful ways—even if some of them resemble or have their roots in traditional or New Age practices—in order to realize that the divine boogies down any and all avenues you create for it.

From Toothpaste to Nightclubs

Praying creatively can be quiet and intimate, or it can be a funked-out, bold burst of self-expression. Who said praying has to be beige? As a creator, your palette is wide open. Carve your own meanings from life's "ordinary" aspects and events; see them with fresh eyes, realize they are chock-full of spiritual potential, and turn them into prayers. This is a way to start stimulating your innate creative sense, how you can begin connecting prayer to your life, and your self to the universe. It's healthy, freeing, and empowering, and it allows prayer to become an endlessly open and spontaneous experience, an ongoing conversation with the divine. Artist Michele Shea says that being creative is a way to be a playmate with the divine. From the seemingly silly to the seriously sacred, your world awaits your creative touch.

45

A large part of creating prayer is not merely responding to things that happen to you ("Please help me get through this break-up") or that you wish would happen to you ("Please help me get into graduate school") but taking initiative and expressing, as authentically and creatively as possible, how you see, touch, taste, smell, hear, and intuit divinity. The divine is alive in your reflection in the bathroom mirror. It lives in the touch of your lover's body. You can feel it between your toes at the beach, taste it in a fresh vegetable, feel it warm your skin as you doze on a sunny day in the park. You can sense it through your physical movements, your intellectual and artistic pursuits, your emotions. So try a few of the 1001 ways to pray:

- Writing a prayer in lipstick across a bathroom mirror
- Drawing it in the sand with your big toe
- Digging it up from the dirt in the woods
- Tattooing it on your skin
- Dancing out a prayer in your living room or at a nightclub, or in the desert
- Releasing it on the keyboard, through a guitar, in a journal, on canvas, on a Web page

Praying creatively is an active and personal manifestation of divinity, a raw and real daily practice, a sacred way of living your life. It's a silly design you draw on the foam of your latte in celebration of quitting your job at Starbucks; your favorite Adrienne Rich poem, which you whisper in your lover's ear when you remember, once again, how much you love him or her; or planting a tomato bush in the old kitchen sink in your backyard because . . . well, just because you felt moved to do so. All are tender interactions with the divine. All are direct modes of communication, creative ways to talk to the universe.

So what, you might be asking, makes these colorful creations and exuberant self-expressions *prayers,* as opposed to just some sort of fun or sensual creative exercise? It's what goes on behind the scenes. Your intent. Your consciousness. Your awareness. John Bunyan, a seventeenth-century minister, said, "In prayer it is better to have a heart without words than words without a heart." Right now, as you read these words, be aware that your life is teeming with divine spark. All you have to do is start recognizing it—and bring some kindling.

⟩ Inspire Yourself ⟨

Here's one way to help you consciously connect your creative self-expressions with the divine, to help you cultivate awareness when you pray:

Try this just before, during, or just after the creation of one of your prayers.

Close your eyes. Breathe slowly, deeply. Still yourself. Let your other senses awaken. Imagine, feel, intuit whatever it is that represents the divine to you. Now, hold this energy for as long as you can. Wrap it around yourself. And carry it with you as you actively create your prayer. If the prayer is already complete, you can simply dedicate your creation, either vocally or silently, to this divine energy. Offer it up. Inspire it. And release it.

47

And remember, it's not necessarily the end result—the painting, or the poem, or the lipstick scrawl—that matters. Often the prayer resides in the act itself; it's in the doing of the thing, consciously and intently, that divinity can shine through. In other words, divine feelings can inspire you to create, or you can create in order to feel divinely inspired. Divinity flows in both directions. Or rather, in all directions. Writer Joseph Chilton Pierce said, "We must accept that this creative pulse within us is God's creative pulse itself."

Need an example of someone who let the divine flow and ignited sacred fires out of the everyday materials of his life? Read on.

Spin Your Prayers

If praying creatively has a role model, someone who embodies its divine and intimate, spiced-up energy most ideally, Persian Sufi mystic Jalaluddin Rumi (1207–1273) is the guy. Rumi was a highly respected, traditional Islamic teacher and scholar who one fine day met a wandering radical mystic named Shamsuddin of Tabriz, and immediately entered into a jumpin' and juicy nontraditional adventure of ecstatic love. The two men spent many delirious weeks together engaged in *sohbet*, mystical communion and discourses. A few of Rumi's family members and students became very jealous of his exclusive relationship with Shams—not to mention more than a bit worried about Rumi's change of lifestyle—so they had Shams run out of town, and when Shams later returned, someone murdered him. (And you thought your relatives were tough.) Needless to say, Rumi was devastated. Out of the intense, almost unbearable separation from his companion, a legendary mystic poet was born.

Amazingly, Rumi had no prior training in classical poetry when he began belting out his profound (and world-famous) musings, yet the verse that emerged from him stands today as some of the most eloquent and beautiful in Persian history. Rumi would spin and dance around a pole in a mosque for hours and hours, singing his pain but also his gratitude for how his relationship with Shams showed him how to intimately experience divine love on earth. From sharing a meal with friends to enjoying a glass of wine, from the feel of his body dancing to the caress of flowers—everywhere he looked, in everything he experienced, Rumi saw evidence of the spiritual love that he and Shams participated in.

Rumi became raw human love caught in divine fire. His prayers burned with sensual honesty and radical self-exposure. His lush phrases married his humanity to divinity. In much of his poetry, it's impossible to tell if Rumi is talking about Shams, himself, or God. All three have been colored red in his love, merged in their meaning and effect, and at their core, are all the same. Here's a short example

☞ Dancing Prayers ☜

Have you ever seen pictures of those beautiful, mystical, white-robed whirling dervishes from Turkey? They're modern-day students of Rumi, imitating his original ecstatic spins, using their bodies and their hearts and souls to express their prayers, to connect with the divine, and to offer thanks.

49

of his verse, but I highly recommend that you pick up any of the translations of Rumi by Coleman Barks or Daniel Ladinsky.

> The minute I heard my first love story
> I started looking for you,
> not knowing
> how blind that was.

> Lovers don't finally meet somewhere.
> They're in each other all along.
> [From *The Essential Rumi,* translations
> by Coleman Barks with John Moyne]

What sets Rumi's prayer-poems apart from most kinds of traditional prayer is that they are openly sensual, even sometimes overtly sexual, as well as mystical. Addressing God as lover or beloved brought Rumi to a unique place in prayer in which he could become as personal, emotional, vulnerable, needy, exhausted, energized, happy, sad, lustful, demure, silly, serious, jealous, or enlightened as any true lover often feels. He whirled, he sang, he tranced, he moaned, he delved into himself and his heart like a man on fire. In short, Rumi let it all hang out.

This honest self-expression is part of what makes Rumi so powerful and his poetry still so popular today. We can all relate to the desire for meaningful union with a loved one (be they a friend, a lover, or the divine) and the immense disappointment of separation that accompanies a divorce, a move, a death, or any dramatic change. Add to the mix such pivotal experiences as a messy breakup, a job

☞ Cry Out Like You Mean It ☜

Don't be afraid or embarrassed to get down and dirty with the divine or to think of divinity in uninhibited, sensual ways or to use sexual terms or to feel erotic sensations when you pray. Hell, saints worldwide have been doing it for centuries. St. Teresa of Avila, Hafiz and Rabi'a in Persia, Mirabai in India, and Julian of Norwich, just to name a few—and, of course, Rumi—all expressed their connection with the divine in not only sensual but sometimes explicitly sexual ways. This kind of openness makes the divine smile, lean in, and pucker its lips. After all, sexual energy is just another form of spiritual energy—and a very potent, delightful one at that.

On the other hand, it's not a requirement. The divine has countless facets, innumerable doors for you to enter. Maybe thinking of the divine as lovingly platonic, paternal or maternal, a best friend, abstract and allusive, silent and still, or even asexual or celibate works best for you. Gandhi said, "Each one prays to God according to his own light." You certainly don't have to be a Rumi. You don't have to be pretty and sensual or use lovely imagery, movements, or lush verbiage when you relate to divinity. You can be as ugly and strange and free as you want. In other words, you don't have to adhere to my or anyone else's use of bodily imagery or sexual language when talking about the divine to be spiritually healthy and attuned. Your approach to igniting your divine spark should be authentic, truthful, and meaningful to you, no matter what it looks or sounds like to others. Now take off your clothes.

lost, a dream unrealized, a sick family member or friend, or just a nasty bout of existential angst, and you've got all the clay you need to mold your prayers. And as Rumi proves, praying out of our pain and our desire can help lingering past wounds and traumas find a healthy exit. But . . . keep in mind that tragedy is not a rule. It's not mandatory for us to encounter some sort of painful, heart-wrenching experience in order to become mystical artists. *All* experiences are potential instigators for praying creatively.

Praying creatively is not a time to worry about grammar or rhythm or coloring inside the lines, or even making sense. Don't be shy. Don't self-censor. You must be daring and unashamed, free of both inhibition and fluff. Trying to keep our selves and our prayers clean and proper and "holy" keeps us separated from them, from our true selves, from connecting with divinity as closely as we can. After all, who would want a prayer that is distant from its giver?

I once heard the wonderful mystic and healer Ron Roth say that the word for *prayer* in Sanskrit (the language of ancient India) is *pal al,* which is best translated as "seeing oneself as wondrously made." He believes that if you're going to effectively communicate with the divine, you must see yourself in this wondrous way. That is exactly the kind of compassionate insight this book intends to help you gain.

Our lives are composed of serious and not-so-serious concerns; we can pray for both big things and little things, and over time and with spiritual growth, we slowly develop the capacity for greater, deeper prayer and greater, deeper wonder. Rumi might have prayed about death and love and God, but you can pray about a haircut.

DON'T BE SHY

DARING AND UNASHAMED

As we all know, a haircut, when backed by the right intention, can be an entirely transformative, divine act. In other words, our prayers should reflect who we are now. You are multifaceted, nuanced, textured. An ever-praying prayer. And, as you will see in the chapter on meditation (Chapter Twelve), prayer isn't all about talking or doing or creating, it's also about listening and just being still with whatever it is that sparks your heart.

Being the Wonder That You Are

All the crispy creation you've read about in this chapter does more than just inspire divine self-knowledge; it actually stimulates the universe at large. The divine manifests itself directly through your creativity; as you express your self, divinity grows and flourishes. It's true. Connecting to and creating with your sacred self quite literally pumps a positive, constructive energy straight into the universe and hence helps the planets orbit, the stars shine, the angels sing, and your world move and grow. Little ol' you can do this? Hell yes. After all, while it may seem like it ain't no big thang to, say, light a candle of thanks to celebrate your new job promotion, it's a very big thang indeed to stimulate this type of harmonious reciprocity and nourish the universe with your ongoing, active participation. Remember, the divine is continuously discovering and recreating itself as it evolves through the course of our human lives. And that means it's our duty not to bore her.

CHAPTER 5

Catapult Your Inner Waitress

Ritualize Your Life; You'll Just Feel Better

All right, so how else can you invoke the divine and actively create a reciprocal relationship with it? One word: rituals. Simply put, a ritual is a dynamic and engaged creative prayer, given a particularly powerful kick through a formalized, symbolic ceremony. Rituals allow us to deliberately set aside time to recognize, honor, and celebrate seminal aspects of life. Birth, death, marriage, holidays—all are traditionally the basis for cultural rituals that are celebrated, in various forms, the world over. Through ritual, we are able to experience, either privately or communally, life's changes, cycles, and history through deliberately marked events. Ritual is a vivid stamp in the soft clay of memory. It's how we talk to time.

Ritual also helps us experience what's called "liminality," a word derived from the Latin *limen,* meaning boundary or threshold. During particularly powerful rituals, participants are able to suspend or cross typical boundaries that separate the sacred from the profane. Anthropologists often call this liminal state the "betwixt and between"—that is, a time and energetic place that is neither here nor there, where traditional norms are dissolved and alternative states can be experienced. Many cultures believe that in this "between" state, we can more directly connect with the divine; therefore, rituals that help provide this sort of link are deeply revered and are often the centerpieces of a culture's spiritual life.

Vision quests, polyphonic chanting, drum circles, masked performances, trance dancing—there are as many varieties of liminal rituals that help people slide from ordinary reality to super-reality and, even, ultimate reality . . . and then back home again as there are cultures of the world. Want more? Here are some examples of traditional rituals that promote an intense experience of the liminal:

- *Sema.* On special occasions—most notably, the anniversary of Rumi's death on December 17—the dervishes gather in a sacred space in Konya, Turkey, and hold a sacred ritual known as *sema.* One by one, the white-robed *semazens* quietly enter a grand hall, leaving behind their normal reality and entering a sacred one. Music is played, and the dervishes begin to slowly whirl and spin around their own central axis. One foot remains in place, while the other pushes the body around and around. The left hand is pointed down to the earth, and the right hand is held palm up and open to the heavens. The dervishes spin for hours on end, inducing a trance-like state wherein they essentially become divine conduits, living energetic channels connecting body with spirit, earth with heaven, human with divine.
- *Peyote rituals.* Peyote, a potent hallucinogenic plant, has been used by many indigenous cultures in the Americas, such as the Huichol Indians of Mexico, for thousands of years. Participants ingest peyote in a carefully monitored ceremony meant to induce super or divine consciousness. Through this sacred ritual, participants remember who they are, where they came from, and why they

57

are here. Dimensions are crossed, realities are shifted, and cultural myths are sustained.

- *Sande.* This female-only initiation ritual, performed by the Mende people of Sierra Leone, represents a girl's sacred transition into womanhood. During Sande, which lasts anywhere from a few days to a few weeks, young women have their entire normal reality upended. They are separated from their family, stripped of their normal clothes, painted in symbolic colors, and taken from their village into the woods to a secret society of older women who teach them everything—from the practical to the magical—that they need to know about womanhood.

When the sacred spinners, the herbally enlightened, and the newly matured females return to ordinary reality, they are forever changed. Some have departed as girls and returned as women; some have experienced irrefutable new proof that Divine and self are One. Some have had a question answered, a vision cleared, a disease healed. Most gain new information and powers, which they share with others (or not) in order to promote a healthier, more divinely aligned life. No matter what the final outcome, all have experienced some acute shift in consciousness.

All well and good, you might say, for the Mende, for the Native Americans, or for spinning Turks who apparently don't suffer motion sickness. But what does this mean for you? Why would you even want to go liminal? Simple: Because when you consciously leave your ordinary, it's a direct invitation to the extraordinary. Unencumbered by typical norms, we are free to allow profound realizations, heightened awareness, and transformative powers to move on in.

And while you can't exactly pick up a bag of peyote down at your local Walgreens, and your studio apartment is probably a mite small for ecstatic whirling, even in your own intimate, modern, funky rituals, you, too, can create the space, the time, the altered liminal state, if you so choose, even without the dramatics, the drums, or the drugs. And no, not every ritual will shoot you into some lofty altered uber-reality; they are not all supposed to. Some rituals are enacted simply to mark a special time, to focus a desire, break a nasty habit, encourage a healthier you, or celebrate a traditional event. There is much to be explored in the betwixt. There is much fun to be had in the between.

Ritualize Your Self

So let's redden ritual a bit more, shall we? Let's make it personal, modern, you. *The Red Book* asks you to create your own rituals—whenever you like, and for any reason whatsoever, as long as they really mean something to you and have some divine weight, some honest tang. Your rituals can be shaped around almost anything at all—like a job promotion or a breakup—or just because you're really craving some divine mojo.

So how do you do it? How do you perform a ritual? Here's a loose general outline, a gleaming skeleton around which to form the flesh of your ideas. Each ritual is unique in its purpose and in its execution. As always, feel free to intermingle, add to, or eliminate these notions as you desire.

1. Choose a specific time and place. The place could be a bedroom, a kitchen, a garage, the beach, the woods, the closet,

the roof. Do not let yourself or other participants be disturbed.

2. Pipe down, focus, ground yourself. (There's more on how to ground in the second half of this book.)

3. Maybe light a candle, or burn some sage or incense—something to give the air some presence, the space some hint of magic and singularity.

4. Once the space is ready, clearly set forth the basic intention of your ritual, out loud or silently, typed on paper, scribbled in hair dye, or in any way you like. For example:

"By burning these sheets, I intend to burn away all negative and unhealthy patterns and people I formerly welcomed into my personal space or bed, like _____ ."

⇌ Burn Clear ⇌

Hindus and Buddhists often burn incense as a way to transport their prayers out to the universe (via the smoke). Many Native people burn bundles of dried sage, or "smudge," to clear a place of negative energy and to purify a space for Spirit to enter. Wiccans light ceremonial candles and create a circle around them in order to protect the space, more clearly direct their intent, and reach altered states of consciousness. Some traditional religions, of course, use candles to symbolize the light of Spirit.

60

5. Burn those sheets! (preferably in a fireplace or some other safe outdoor space and not, as you might be fantasizing, on the hood of your ex-boyfriend's Jetta), saying something like, "I now welcome only positive, healthy energy and people into my personal space and bed. These new sheets will be blessed and will remind me of my intent." (Sound good? Too cheesy? Make it as serious or funky, as profound or edgy as you like. Just make sure it really means something to you.)

6. Put those brand new, blessedly positive, intention-soaked sheets on your bed.

7. Douse the various fires, thus marking your return to the ordinary, and release your intention, the ritual, your prayer, to the fates . . . and tell any freaked-out firemen they can go home now.

⮚ Spatulas Are Welcome Here ⮘

What to bring: Rituals often involve lots of accoutrements—flowers, photos, crystals, icons, food offerings, candles, incense, chanting, music—all of which are great, time-honored implements for marking ritual time and place. But *The Red Book* is not about restricting you to the traditional. Bring the "tools" or items that most connect you to the ritual you are performing, whatever they are, even if they seem random: credit cards, body lotion, a spatula, a car tire, your diploma, a vibrator, vitamins, bed sheets. Ya gotta go with what feels right to you.

61

Catapult Your Inner Waitress

Need more? Here are some examples of inspired modern rituals I've encountered that really resonated with the participants:

- A yoga instructor I know once got together with a few of her close friends—all former or current waitresses—and they decided, as many waitresses invariably do, that they needed someone else to take of their special orders. So they lit the candles and poured the wine and gathered the materials and built their very own effigy of a waitress, made of wood and cloth, right down to the last detail. They dressed her in a genuine waitress uniform and gave her a notepad, on which they all placed their respective orders: a new job, a husband, a health issue cleared, a book published, a mother returning, a fearless change of perspective.

    They carried their effigy to the beach that very night, gathered around, and, with a huge ceremonial yell, catapulted their sacrificial (and yes, completely biodegradable) waitress out to sea, to the great divine cosmic kitchen, where there are no rude customers, no lousy tips, no sore spiritual ankles. Then they all cheered, and laughed, and high-fived, and went back for more wine.

- A dear friend of mine was having a hard time getting over a breakup. She woke up one morning, lit some honey incense, stared at herself in the mirror for a while, and conjured up all the memories of her past relationship. Then she picked up some scissors and proceeded to chop off her long hair. With every snip, she felt her old perceptions dropping to the floor. Then she swept up all the pieces of her past, which no longer supported her present, and threw them into the garbage. She is a proud, powerful pixie now. And she's never looked better.

• One of my most sacred personal rituals involved my marriage—to myself. During one particularly wobbly, transitional period of my life, a dear friend and I rented a tiny cabin near some natural hot springs. During the evening, I lit two small candles, sat down on the hardwood floor, and said my pre-written vows to myself, with my friend as a witness. I said that I was marrying my higher self. That I would never abandon it, no matter who or what came into my life. That I would stay conscious and nourish my power, my voice, my truth. That I was deeply committed to my self from this day forward. I said this all aloud. Clearly. Deeply. With all my heart. The entire ritual took about two minutes. Then I blew out the candles, and went to bed.

Maybe these examples strike you as a bit too New Age-y or witchy or just too damn Californian. Or maybe they seem more heavily ritualistic than you want for your praying. No problem. For those who experienced them—we, who are not witches or New Agers and only a few of whom live in California—these rituals felt organic and authentic. And not every ritual has to be a dramatic, mind-boggling, life-altering event. You can easily set up small daily rituals that still involve you and the divine sitting down together for an honest touch. Perhaps your ritual is resting under that gorgeous old willow tree in the park on your lunch break or standing at the corner or in your bedroom around 3 A.M. on those nights when the moon hits you just right. Or perhaps when you dance with divine intent around your living room to the new Moby CD, you'll hear the answer to your question about whether you should change jobs. When you take that healing ritual bath, perhaps all that toxic self-blame for your parents' divorce will begin to drain away. When you share a special meal with friends or family once a week, perhaps you'll simply feel more nourished, loved, in right relation with the life you are choosing and the community around you. In fact, you probably already practice many rituals but may not recognize them as such. In that case, maybe it's time to crank up the intent behind them. All it takes is a little conscious attention, a little divine connection.

Something to keep in mind: It can be easy to get so caught up in, say, the pretty flower arrangements for your marriage ritual that you miss the real, inner ritual that needs to be taking place, arm in arm with the external. Rituals without personal roots, without deep consciousness and core connection, will just be speed bumps on your path, whereas rituals performed with presence, responsibility, intent, love, and creative soulfire are rocket rides to another level of being.

Another key point: While the effects of ritual can be immediate, more often than not they are slow in their revelation. For instance, after I married myself (Did I mention that a few friends even sent me wedding cards? And that I bought myself a funky ring?), I definitely did not wake up the next morning all enlightened and honeymooned. But over the following months, I did notice a subtle but powerful change and began to quietly appreciate all the ways this commitment to my self affected my life.

Part of the change was that I became much more active. I paid more attention. I became more aware of when, where, and to whom

Creative SOULFIRE

I might be giving away my power—for example, during that class I took every Tuesday with that intimidating teacher whose views I would always let override my own intuition. I became more conscious of when I shut my self down or compromised my integrity. I spent more time doing the things that fed my soul: dancing, re-reading my favorite books, watching dogs play on the beach, journaling, visiting places I'd always wanted to see, hanging out with loved ones, and, most important, just being still. I said "no" more often when I felt I needed time alone—no matter how incredible the party sounded. My ritual had initiated these changes, but I had to keep putting fuel in my tank. The point is to put the energy out there, to light that first twig in the bonfire and then keep stirring the pot. The rest will unfold in due time.

Altar Your Self

Surely you've noticed that colorful little Shiva shrine at the back of your favorite Indian restaurant? Or maybe the smiling Buddha sitting at the entrance to the Asian market, surrounded by candles and pennies? How about those flower-laden Madonna statuettes adorning countless church nooks? From yoga studios to your Italian grandmother's bedroom, altars are everywhere.

And no one says they have to be strictly traditional. An altar can take any shape or form your divine imagination desires: a coffee table or a tree trunk, a shoebox or a microwave oven, set up in a distinct, semi-private space, like a corner of your bedroom or kitchen, part of the backyard, or behind that silk Chinese screen in your living room. No matter where you create it, a personal altar can provide a specific focus for your prayers, a spiritual nucleus around which to swirl your intent, your unique personality, and your love, not to mention some magically delicious transformational energies. (In fact, the word *focus* is Latin for "fireplace" or "altar.")

And what, you might ask, do you actually put on an altar? Power objects. Symbols, icons, photos, poems, rocks, fruit, jewelry, a small glass of wine—anything that resonates with you personally and represents what is nurturing to your spirit at this moment. *Mana* is a Polynesian word and idea that represents power, meaning, life force. Things that have cultural or personal significance in Polynesia—like certain mountains, spiritual icons, or a sport star's baseball—are all thought to have *mana*. So what has *mana* for you?

Maybe it's that goosebump-inducing verse from your favorite spiritual book, a goofy-sweet picture of the Dalai Lama, or a smooth stone from your favorite vacation spot, accompanied by candles and flowers for ambiance and beauty. Altars are all about concrete, tangible reminders, physical souvenirs from a spiritual path that can sometimes feel very abstract and fuzzy. Have fun blurring the line that separates the sacred from the profane, and remember to spill your daily life directly onto your altar. Your grad school acceptance letter, pregnancy test results, that particularly hilarious valentine, a plane ticket, a picture of your childhood dog, your grandmother's pearls, your first nose ring—all are altar-riffic. Your altar can be an ornate, elaborate creation, brimming over with vivid color and vanilla candles. Or it can consist of a single twig, carefully placed. No matter what you adorn it with, remember to keep it

66

moving. Like you, an altar is an ever-evolving creation. The displays in your altared vision should morph as you do.

The objects you're altaring should ignite the divine both inside and outside of you and should remind you of why you are on this path of spiritual discovery in the first place. They should open your heart and raise your consciousness—and maybe your mother's eyebrows. They should empower you. Move you to pray. And not be too flammable. And please, treat your altar space with respect. Keep it fresh, clean, and revered. Don't put empty Pizza Hut boxes or old copies of *Elle* on it—unless those are somehow sacred to you (and if they are, well, more power to you, sister). Don't let just anybody mess with your altar. It's not a dollhouse. Don't let it become a fashion statement for your friends (hey, check out how spiritual I am). Please. Keep it real. These are not merely cute art projects. These are powerful spaces where you invoke the divine, blessed nooks where the divine is evoking you, so be sure to hold a clear intention about your space.

Altars are personal, concentrated energy centers, places to visit when you're craving an energetic buzz, when you need a space to vent, or when you're just seeking some peace of mind. And of course, they are the perfect place to perform some of your most intimate, powerful rituals, or even the simpler daily ones. Try lighting a candle or burning some lavender incense on your altar every morning, signaling a new beginning, a new day, a quiet time for self-reflection. Or maybe you have an inspiring poem you can read aloud, a chant you can hum, a visualization or meditation you can practice. Try journaling in front of your altar, dreaming next to it, or dancing on top of it. Want more ideas? Check the resource section in the back of this book for some terrific reference guides on creating these intimate, consecrated spaces. Otherwise, find a quiet corner, gather the precious materials in your life, and altar away.

Here's Looking at You, Kid

Spirituality is not just about trying to see the divine in all things but is also about getting the divine to see all of you—which, in another sense, means getting you to see all of you. And guess what? Creative prayer just happens to be the perfect medium for this type of sacred reciprocity.

Hindus perceive a special, interpersonal exchange between devotee and divinity that they call *darsan* (pronounced "dar-shawn"). It means, simply, both seeing and being seen by the divine, with a quite literal emphasis on the "being seen" element. In Hinduism, sacred images (like those you might keep on your altar) and holy people (even photos or statues of them) are not considered separate from the divine; they are a direct manifestation of divinity. As such, if you ever visit an Indian holy place, you'll doubtless see hundreds, even thousands of devotees pushing and shoving and jockeying for position, trying not only to catch a glimpse of a divine icon or mystic but to actually put themselves in her direct line of sight. Hi there! I see you, you see me, we are relating.

The Red Book shamelessly appropriates this marvelously powerful notion. After all, you want divinity to know you're conscious of your important role in existence, right? But the catch is, you gotta

want to be seen. So become a divine exhibitionist. Play more, laugh more, do things that make your spirit roar, that amplify all your senses and encourage others to smile. Love boldly. Make your spirituality brighter, your prayers more colorful, your life more refined and reflective. Not only make the divine see you, but make the divine want to lick your forehead and taste you. After all, it's not enough to merely notice the divinity in the oak tree or gorgeous sunset or in your feelings for your loved ones, or even in the mirror. You have to pray from such an honest and open and raw place in yourself that the divine eagerly wants to kneel at the altar of you.

CHAPTER 6

Divine Winks
The Universe Wants
Your Attention.
Will You Wink Back?

The divine is slapping your ass right now. It happened yesterday. It will continue tomorrow, even if you try to avoid it. Yes, this is a positive thing, a magical and fine-tuned phenomenon, one that is so much more beneficial with your conscious participation. At this point in *The Red Book*, igniting a relationship with the divine turns into a more immediate practice, as it requires cultivating a way of perceiving the world by using what spiritual teacher Caroline Myss calls "symbolic sight," the practice of recognizing that everything around you, all the everyday stuff in your world, exudes spiritual power and illumination. It's all rich in information and clues, all aimed directly at you. Your responsibility, then, is to become open enough to see these winks; to learn how to decipher the hints and unpack the symbolic information; and then, of course, to boldly wink back.

Learning to use symbolic sight helps you move through your seemingly chaotic life with more grace and ease and less bumbling and stumbling. It's like having spiritual Cliffs Notes on your unique life drama. It's reading between the lines and seeing the meaning behind the mayhem. Observing your life through the universe's eyes makes nothing coincidental and everything pure potential. As the Zen saying goes, "No snowflake ever falls in the wrong place." So let's first look at how using symbolic sight can help you better receive the answers to your specific prayers, and then we'll focus on

being aware of the signs and symbols the universe is chucking at you left and right, whether you're praying for them or not.

Answer My Damn Prayer Already

Know this: Once a prayer has been created, ritualized, altared, danced, sung, imagined, moaned, or breathed, it has already been received. But what about those times when your prayers involve some serious, direct questions, which demand specific responses? What if there's something you just really want or really need to know?

Well, *The Red Book* firmly believes that if you ask the divine for a response or a solution, you'll invariably get it. Always. That's right, *always*. Ask and ye shall receive. But here's the catch: It's often incredibly tricky and sometimes damn annoying to try to hear the answers. Because the answer almost never comes in a form we expect, we often swear we've heard no answer at all. Sad but true. Examples? There are plenty:

• Let's say you pray for a creative, fulfilling job. Soon an amazing position opens at one of your favorite companies, and you're sure this is the answer to your prayers. You apply, you interview, and it all goes beautifully. But you don't get the job. You are flabbergasted and stunned. At the same time, your friend offers you a lowly temp job at her company. You're more than a little peeved with the supposedly generous universe you've read about, because you're sure your prayer has been ignored and you've been reduced to filing receipts and cleaning the coffeemaker. You start browsing atheistsarecool.com.

Three months later, lo and behold, you are offered an even better job than that original dream gig, through someone you met at the temp job. You also read in the *Times* that the company offering the original position turned out to be under investigation by the SEC for stock fraud and just went bankrupt. You realize that if you had landed that job, the one that looked so ideal at the time, not only would you have missed this even better opportunity, but hey, you might be in prison right now. And you know how you hate the baggy peach jumpsuit look.

• Exhausted from seemingly endless battles with anxiety, you pray to find someone to help you heal. Weeks go by, and you keep your eyes and ears open, but you receive no referrals to magical acupuncturists from your yoga teacher, no self-help books cut it, and no one mentions "the most fabulous therapist ever" at any of the dinner parties you attend.

However . . .

you've begun to spend your Saturdays with that wonderful elderly widow who just moved into the apartment above you. She makes you herbal teas, and you read her romance novels. She feeds you homemade soups, and you take her for long walks in the park. You listen to her hilarious stories, and she pats your tummy when you cry.

Now, ask yourself: Did you find a healer or not?

Here's the gist: You gotta drop your normal expectations of how a prayer is supposed to be answered. Pray honestly, clearly, with full intent, and then release your prayer, along with your attachment to what form the answer should take. Abolishing expectations allows

Read between the lines

for all possibilities of response. Pay attention to everything that shows up. Poke it, undress it, really look at it before you huff and puff and blow it all away.

The trick is that even though answers often arrive in ways you didn't expect, they're almost invariably better than what you asked for, even though—and this is an extremely important point—*it might not seem like it at the time.* It requires a well-tuned sort of insight to read between the spiritual lines, to understand that the divine delivers in its own way *and* in its own time. Call it "divine time"—sort of like "island time," only with a wholly different kind of lip-smacking margarita on tap.

Connecting the Dots

It can get convoluted. Sometimes we want or pray for what we genuinely are ready for, but it comes in a package we were not expecting, so we disregard it and miss the prince hiding in the frog. Or more often, we pray for what we are actually *not* ready for, so we miss what we actually need, the necessary steps or lessons that will lead us to what we want. We want G right now, when in fact the divine is offering us A through F first, so that we can really appreciate G.

Here's a classic example: At one point or another, nearly every woman I know has prayed (intensely, passionately) for true love to show up—like, you know, *right now*—or at least before the next high school reunion. Most of us have spent endless hours imagining this person, perhaps performing little love rituals, and asking, over and over again, "Where the hell is my dream guy?" as we eagerly await the universe's answer. But what shows up instead? A nasty inferiority complex, courtesy of a new lover whom we know, deep down, is definitely *not* our One True Love. Or maybe we get something completely unexpected, like a forced relocation or a lengthy business trip to Nepal (hey, it could happen). What the hell sort of divine answers are those?

Here is where you really begin to read between those spiritual lines. Try shifting your perspective to see how these experiences might actually be a different sort of answer, like hieroglyphs to be decoded, each designed to build you up and strengthen your spirit in ways you might not even recognize yet. These experiences could very well turn out to be key foundations for your temple of *luuv*. Maybe the sudden heightened inferiority complex disturbs you so much that you are finally willing to face your unhealthy emotional habits, such as that tendency to choose lovers that reflect your lack of self-respect or your fears of being alone. Perhaps traveling to Nepal empowers you in a way that no trip to Cabo ever could, because you learn how to travel by yourself in an entirely different culture and become much more courageous, confident, self-sufficient, and open-minded. Not to mention the amazing guy you meet on the plane trip home.

If we allow their lessons to come through, the seemingly bizarre or unrelated answers that come into our lives will usually help us to attract the deep, true love relationships we've prayed so hard for. Eventually. After all, like attracts like: If you want the real deal, you have to become the real deal yourself. So when your next lover does finally arrive and you ask the universe if this, at long last, is your dream guy, the universe simply reflects the question right back to you: Are you your dream girl?

Remember, each event in our lives is not an end in itself. The events are all just part of something greater. Every act, every decision is a choice, a move that informs the next one, and every single choice you make transforms you, either a little or a lot, along with everyone else involved. So even if you can't grasp the whole picture immediately, keep trusting the steps being presented to you. Life is like a funky game of connect the dots, and most of the time, you can only connect those dots by looking backward.

This Will Totally Freak You Out

And then there are those all-too-frequent times when we fully see the answer to our prayers right in front of us, but we want to hide from it. Why? Because most of the time, the answer requires us to change, to become more responsible in our life, to get off our butt and start creating a more authentic life. And this can scare the crap out of us. As the saying goes, be careful what you wish for; you just might get it. Two examples:

One night you attend an art exhibit that deeply inspires you to send off an emotionally charged, body-tingling prayer for the universe to help you finally fulfill your dream of becoming an artist. Weeks fly by, and you don't do anything about your passionate artistic yearnings. Six months later, you suddenly get fired from your cubicle job. You are mighty pissed, to say the least.

Now, you realize that you might have created this situation through your prayer and intent, but you're still totally ticked that this might be an answer, because it didn't exactly arrive in a timely way or on a silver platter (for example, waiting for you to find the spare time to create your artistic masterpiece, which is immediately placed in the Guggenheim, which makes you rich and famous so you can *then* quit your job) but is instead offering you the chance to go fill your own platter. Now. Either you can ignore the answer to your prayer and feel sorry for yourself and watch endless reruns of *Desperate Housewives,* or you can fill in the rest of that divine answer and recreate your life so that it supports your passion for artistic expression. The choice, as always, is yours.

Or . . .

one day you watch an exceptional *Oprah* episode, all about the power of love and forgiveness, and you feel deeply moved and inspired. So you pray for major heart opening, for the chance to really learn to love like you never have before. You spend all the next afternoon daydreaming about hanging out with Mother Teresa in heaven, when suddenly your own mother calls. Her house has flooded, and she needs to camp out in your tiny apartment . . . for a month. You do not get along with your mother, and you consider creating an elaborate excuse—something about Borneo and contagious mold—to explain why this is just impossible right now. But then it hits you. *Oprah.* Love. Oh, shit.

Yes indeed, here is part of your answer. Now you have to face your mother, someone who represents an entirely different aspect of love than you were expecting. Here indeed is part of your learning about how to love more deeply, the reality of spiritual life, and the hidden "gifts" of prayer. See? Isn't this fun?

To put it bluntly, the universe is not your bitch. The divine does not hand out complete answers all tied up in pretty ribbons;

it is your partner, not your personal Santa Claus. Again, most of us hide from the responses to our prayers because they demand change—emotional, physical, or some other kind. And let's face it, change freaks us out. It takes guts to pray creatively, but it takes even more guts to be able to truly see, understand, and act responsibly on the answers we receive.

I Am So Not Worthy

All of this talk of divine guidance may bring up a negatively charged question you might secretly be asking: Am I worthy? Do I and my weird/mundane/messy little life, with my petty prayers for a new relationship or a great job or healthier self-esteem, deserve such attention from the divine, when the world is full of, well, tsunamis and hurricanes and poverty and war and AIDS and a million other epic dramas that seem to be much more dire and deserving of the divine's time? Short answer: Hell yes, you deserve it. Longer answer: While those global issues are indeed extremely prayer-worthy and in need of as much healing energy as you can beam their way, so is *every* aspect of your life, no matter how seemingly small or shallow. Understand this: The divine does not make such distinctions. You cannot ask for more than you deserve. This is impossible, because there is no holy sliding scale of need, no giant measuring cup of worthiness gauging who gets how much divine sauce based on some sort of impossible, guilt-laden criterion.

Remember, the divine is an all-pervasive energy force that resides in and affects all things in all places at all times, and you are just as much a part of it (and it of you) as any other creature on the planet. The amount of divine energy in the world is not finite. You cannot use it up. You cannot chop it into tiny pieces. You cannot diminish its volume. You can only add to it and join it and allow it in—or block its presence in your life. So then the question becomes not, Do I deserve it? but rather, *How can I use it better?* And truly, if more of us started acting from (instead of against) the divine guidance running rampant through our lives, even in seemingly small ways, we probably would not have the poverty and wars and AIDS epidemics we do now. And believe it or not, we also might not have the tsunamis, but let's save the funkier metaphysics for *The Blue Book*.

Sign Language

But what about the times when you're not actively praying for something? Does the divine just sort of shut up and humbly recede behind the curtains of your life? No way, José. The universe is *constantly* communicating with you, offering messages and ideas and nudges through tangible signs, symbols, numbers, colors, strangers, and natural phenomena. Albert Einstein said, "My religion consists of a humble admiration of the illimitable superior spirit who reveals himself in the slight details we are able to perceive . . ."

Let's get a bit more specific: A sentence the bus driver mumbles, an errand you have to run for your boss, the graphic designer sitting next to you on the plane, that strange bird that perches on your bench in the park, a TV commercial, the color of that woman's purse—they're all rich in divine potential. See, that bus driver might utter just the right words to jump-start your decision to change

80

jobs, or the hot red color of that woman's purse might remind you of the color of the sky in that wildly archetypal dream you had the night before, or that seemingly random errand you run for your boss might run you right into your old best friend, whom you haven't seen for ten years, resulting in a heartfelt reunion that is so very needed at this time in your life. Here are a few typical ways that the universe waves at you:

- Information, ideas, words spoken by other people, like something a character says on TV, or a song on the radio, or the way your iPod randomly hits that certain song, with those certain lyrics, at that most appropriate time
- Words or phrases that leap out at you from magazines, newspapers, shampoo bottles, cereal boxes, Web pages, license plates, bumper stickers, and books (especially when a book slips off a shelf or falls open to a "random" page)
- Stranger-than-normal happenings, like when your car won't start when you're planning to drive by your ex-boyfriend's house again (for, like, the seventh time that week) or you lose your wallet when you're about to bid on a pair of "authentic" Jimmy Choo sandals on eBay or your Internet connection crashes right when you're about to send that certain e-mail to your boss
- Signs—*real* signs, like billboards, advertisements, street signs, even traffic lights or construction signs—that flash you a phrase or keyword or icon that happens to match up in some striking way with what's going on in your life or in your heart
- Seemingly coincidental patterns, like overhearing four different people mention the same book or yoga class or discuss the

same political idea or vitamin supplement or spiritual teacher in the same week

Paying attention to how the universe tweaks your nose will liven up even the most boring subway ride and will constantly remind you that the divine is always there; I mean, here; I mean, both in You and out of You and as You and as Him and as Her and as that dog and as that color and as that piece of sushi and . . . well, you get the idea.

Is That a Divine Sign or Just a Parking Ticket?

Yes, it takes practice to discern which are signs from the universe and which are just, well, not. Like when you've heard about that certain vitamin supplement six times in one week and then, later, it catches your eye in the health food store. Is that something to be expected, or is it a sign? A little confusion is understandable because, let's face it, as young women, we're constantly being hit, and hit hard, with *thousands* of suggestions, urges, and commands to buy this and wear that and be this and do that now or else, and if we're not careful, these distractions can drone out the more divinely coordinated signs, those that match our unique souls, the ones specifically designed to help us gain clarity instead of extra, well, stuff. So check in. See what resonates. Be aware of a certain subtle but steady tingling or heart-fluttering, a deep intuitive knowing that usually accompanies divine signs.

heart-fluttering

But please don't worry too much about misreading signs at the beginning. What's most important for now is just opening yourself up to divine possibility. Allow yourself to see signs about anything and everything, even if you think you must be totally making it up when "Just Do It" appears on TV at the exact moment you are questioning whether you should audition for that play.

At the beginning, it's OK to pretend, if it helps things get moving and frees you from doubt. Sometimes it's necessary to act on most hunches and signs you get, even if they don't result in much, just so you learn to crank up your receptors and relax your expectations. Over time, you'll naturally become more adept at discerning which signs are divine signs and which signs may be neurosis, or wishful thinking, or just a cop needing to fill her ticket quota.

Your Lucky Number

When I notice a particular symbol or color or person or word or number or force of nature showing up in my life more frequently than normal, sometimes I'll sit down and list all my personal associations with the sign or, if it feels right, I'll do some research and investigate what that word or symbol might mean in other cultures or religions. Kabbalah (the Jewish mystical school of thought), alchemy, and many other esoteric spiritualities—and even some traditional world religions—all believe in the hidden powers and spiritual significance of numbers (aka numerology), colors, letters, and certain names, dates, and images. Plenty of excellent books

⇌ Paint Your Own Signs ⇌

You don't always have to wait around to see what the universe dishes up; it's great to set your own sign-meter and tell the universe, "OK, whenever I see that TV commercial, it's gonna remind me to pursue my acting passion" or "Whenever I see a MINI Cooper, I will quiet my ego" or "Whenever I see 11:11 on a digital clock, it will signal a little divine wave, a little yahoo from the universe, a little reminder to take a deep breath and pay attention to the right now." The possibilities are endless.

Personally, whenever I have some question churning in my mind and can't quite get a grasp on what to do, I ask the universe (and set an intention) for some guidance, and I simply take a walk. I just relax and keep myself grounded and open, and see if anything stands out. A bird, a person, a strange interaction, a sudden brainstorm, a license plate, or anything. What's fascinating is that once we start really paying attention to signs, they seem to become more frequent and juicier, more meaningful. In other words, the more you do it, the more it seems to happen. It's like opening a divine valve.

exist on everything from numerology to sacred geometry to the alchemical process. There's nothing that says you can't become an intrepid symbologist yourself (not an actual profession, by the way, but after the incredible success of *The Da Vinci Code*, it really should be), one who's not afraid to dig a little in order to learn a lot.

But you need to do more than just research. You need to *respond*. You need to *act,* to walk your symbol's talk. Is the number seven popping up like crazy in your life lately, so much that it gets your intuitive attention? Excellent. Twenty minutes of research will tell you that according to a whole range of traditions, seven is considered a powerfully mystical number. It took seven days to create the universe in Genesis; there are seven heavens in Islam and seven chakras in the human body; and to the Pythagoreans, seven represented female enchantment (yay!). So what do you do the next time you're out looking for a new pad and you find one building you really love and you're offered your choice of apartment #4 or apartment #7? What feels like the right choice? Which way has the universe been nudging you? And won't it be nice when you find out later that apartment #4 has leaky faucets that drip all night and neighbors who play country music till 3 A.M. and something that smells really funny in the closet? This is how you wink back at the universe. Does this mean that every sign you follow will result in immediate gratification or that you should act blindly on every seven that pops up from here on out? Of course not. Use your head; pay attention to what resonates. And know that some signs you follow are like wine; they get better with time.

Not Another Butterfly Tattoo

Keep in mind that not every sign calls for some sort of physical action; instead, some might nudge you toward some sort of profound *internal* realization. I remember the morning, years ago, when I had to say my final good-byes to my high school boyfriend before we left for our separate colleges. I was utterly heartbroken and miserable and definitely *not* specifically praying for guidance; I was just too pissed off at the universe for allowing me to go through such unnecessary pain. As I pulled out of my driveway to drive to his apartment one last time, I noticed dark thunderclouds overhead, heralding a ferocious summer storm that was about to break loose. Great. Just then, a large monarch butterfly fluttered right across my windshield. Something in me snapped, and I stopped the car and just bawled my eyes out even more, because I believed this poor little creature was definitely gonna get totally wiped out by the storm, a fact that just added to my general pissed-offness. Yeah, I was in a bad place.

A few hours later, after the violent storm and after my heart-wrenching, runny-nosed farewell to my boyfriend, I pulled back into my driveway, and at the exact same place, a large monarch flew right across my windshield in the opposite direction from before. I stopped my car and watched it fly away. The butterfly was OK. It made it. It had survived the storm, and in fact, it looked pretty strong. My body tingled. My heart beat louder. Time stood still. This little sign had a surprising, deeply healing impact on me. From that point forward, I was more comfortable with moving on.

I later learned about the astounding migratory journeys of the monarchs. These delicate yet resilient creatures fly all the way from Canada to Mexico and back, every year, and most of them survive the most violent storms and extreme conditions imaginable, making these seemingly fragile creatures some of the most mysterious and strong in the insect world. I also learned that according to many mythologies, butterflies represent transformation and change—two constants in life that I often resist—and so I decided that this wonderfully resilient little orange creature would become one of my personal symbols, a totem animal for me. To this day, it's amazing how often a monarch will flit across my vision right when a major change is occurring in my life, sometimes fluttering through the bushes in the park, drawn on a little girl's notebook, tattooed on the sacrum of the woman in front of me in yoga class, or even floating through my dreams. The monarchs appear, maybe as a warning, maybe as an encouragement, and most definitely as a tangy reminder of my inner strength and my ability to let change happen, to release the old and let myself transform into something new.

Natural Elements

Famed inventor and botanist George Washington Carver once said, "I love to think of nature as an unlimited broadcasting station, through which God speaks to us every hour, if we will only tune in." In almost all cultures of the world—especially those of indigenous peoples and earth-based religions—nature is viewed as a deeply symbolic and powerful way that the divine communicates with humans. Mountains, trees, rivers; stars and planets (astrology, anyone?); seasons and elements all have profoundly symbolic significance.

Take, for just one example, the moon: According to myriad Western European neopagan traditions, waxing moons have often been regarded as times for adding new things, ideas, projects, and people to your life, whereas waning moons provide just the right energy for letting go of the things in your life that are not serving your well-being anymore. The moon is often believed to be feminine, opposing the masculine sun, and is associated with intuition, mystery, and hidden powers. It's a potent fertility symbol and regulates female menstrual cycles, gravity, and tides. Just for starters.

The Loud Annoying Crow in the Park

Many cultures, such as those of the Native Americans, believe strongly in totems—that is, in animal spirits or nature beings that align with and assist humans. Animals, even the mangier ones that roam the cities, have an extraordinary way of reflecting back to us what is happening in our lives and often offer symbolic support and guidance. Take a look around your life and note any animals— live ones or those in pictures or movies or in your dreams or on T-shirts—that tend to frequent your vision and that resonate with you. Maybe crows, which are oh-so-common and which you might see almost every day, for whatever reason, give you an extra zing just now. Don't dismiss them due to their commonness. Observe. Listen. Learn. Do a little research. Perhaps their eating schedule or mating habits or their beautiful black feather color will sync up with some part of your life and, combined with their overall spiritual and mythological significance (crows, for example, are considered to be protectors, prophets, and symbols of creativity), will give you a few hints or lessons to implement in your life.

Have you ever been chased by a squirrel? Intensely stared at by a dog? Awakened from a dream or nap by a vociferous bird? Take a moment, try to focus, and see what or whom you were just musing about or what you were feeling right before the critter got feisty. Spiritual teacher Ted Andrews says in *Animal-Speak*, "Nature speaks to us if we listen. Every animal has a story to tell. Every flower blossoms with reminders to be creative, and every tree whispers with its rustling leaves the secrets of life" (p. ix). I highly recommend that you peruse his informative books, which are listed in the Select Bibliography. You'll never look at that crow, or tree, or squirrel in quite the same way again. And this is a good thing.

My Perfect Shade of Red

Despite my undying zeal for research (if you haven't noticed by now, I'm a tireless info digger and gatherer of data on myriad things that interest me), I'm also careful not to allow another's experience of a given symbol or sign define my experience. For instance, in some spiritualities and cultures, the color red, the key word in the title of this very book and the initial inspiration for igniting my own divine spark, is not always considered, vibrationally speaking, the "highest" color of the spectrum. Some spiritual systems see red as the color of the base chakra (the "lowest" of the seven basic energy centers of the human body and the one that supports our survival instinct). Red can also represent overidentification with ego, war, anger, aggression, Communism, the planet Mars, and other not so spiritually enlightened things. But I tend to think these are more patriarchal definitions and experiences of red, and I feel it's time to reclaim it. In China, red means joy. In India, Hindu brides wear red to symbolize fertility and the mother goddess herself is often represented as red in color, symbolizing the principle of creation itself—the active, dynamic principle of feminine power often referred to as *Shakti.* Now, *that's* more like it.

To me, red is the intuitive pulse that beats between reason and blind faith. It's the color of blood when given some air. It activates a passionate, feminized mysticism. It reminds me of a compassionate heart, transformative fire, mystical embodiment, boundless love, self-empowerment, Mary Magdalene's hair, Kali's tongue, my favorite purse, and belly laughs. This color works beautifully for me at this time in my life, but it might not for you. Likewise, a butterfly might not represent transformation for you and the number seven may not feel sacred to you in the slightest, despite its traditional spiritual significance. And that's fine, that's good, that saves the world from one more butterfly tattoo. What does speak to you? What color, what animal, what number or symbol or tree or insect or sound or smell? Tune in to the world around you, and find out.

It's a Sign of Dependency

I remember, one morning when I was about eight years old, planting a seed in my friend's backyard and telling everyone that God would turn it into a full-grown flower by the next morning. (I know, I was just your ordinary, bored suburban kid, looking for some attention.) I was a good convincer; I had all the neighborhood kids believing it, and I felt I could absolutely *prove* God's magical existence with this irrefutable sign. Of course, the next morning there was nothing there but dirt, and the kids were disappointed and the adults sympathetic, and of course, I felt (sniff) abandoned by God and briefly considered throwing a massive tantrum. But then I noticed the little three-year-old girl from across the street, who had come out to hear what all the commotion was about. And what was she holding in

90

her chubby little hand? Yep, a flower. I got it. The lesson here: Watch out for becoming overly attached to signs and overly dependent on receiving them.

One last thing: Please don't think, "Now that I'm more divinely attuned, I'm not having a baby/moving to Rio/going for my Ph.D. unless I receive a sure-fire sign from the universe." This just denies your own inner knowing and essentially gives away your power and spiritual authority to something outside of you. Don't sit back and wait for the doorbell to ring before you move. Go ahead and ring it yourself. Remember: Nudges from the universe are not necessarily being done (or not being done) *to* you; you are, instead, *a partner in their creation,* and hence, *you* determine their presence and their consequences. And by the way, this divine exchange, the winks and signs and answers to your prayers, don't just happen when your eyes are wide open but also when your eyes are wide shut.

TRANSFORMATIVE Fire

CHAPTER 7

Dream On
Widening the Spotlight
in Your Internal Theater

We've all done it. Called our friends in the morning all groggy and gasping, "I had *the* most bizzaro dream last night. I was in some sort of twisted dance contest with my old boss—except he didn't really look anything like my old boss—and a pink cat and my refrigerator, which had really tiny feet and was wearing those new cool Pumas we ooohed at yesterday. Anyway, the cat won and demanded that my boss and I lick the refrigerator clean, but my tongue froze to the Dijon mustard jar, and so then the cat and my boss started making ham and pickle sandwiches using my tongue. So, uh, what do ya think that's about?" Ah yes, from the sensationally psychedelic to the achingly sublime, dreams are yet another fantabulous way that the divine caresses your world.

When we sleep, our unconscious mind can go for a romp and shake off some of its daylight limits. Dreams enable us to receive divine winks as well as catch intriguing glimpses of our ego personality in a space where we are not as quick to shut down or deny what is wanting to be healed or realized as we are in everyday life. *The Red Book* believes that these hazy late-night gambols with your unconscious, if heeded and acted upon, will begin to, well, wake you up to your divine self.

Obviously, not every dream is loaded with mystical symbolism or divine paddle whacks, but if you take time to interpret those that seem to have a richer palette of meanings, you'll find that many

dreams act as impressive mirrors or guides. Rich with signs and symbols, archetypes and metaphors, dreams usually are not to be taken literally but are to be absorbed, unfolded, respectfully interpreted, and never quickly dismissed or underestimated. After all, they are yet another significant, though slightly hazy language that the divine speaks, one in which you can become fluent, so as to translate lessons and sacred wisdom into your waking life.

⇒ Did You Know? ⇒

- Everyone dreams several times a night, and most dreams last five to twenty minutes.
- We will each spend a grand total of about six years dreaming during our lifetime.
- People who have been blind since birth still have dreams.
- If you're snoring, you're not dreaming (and if you're near a snorer, you probably aren't, either).
- *Lucid dreaming* means being aware that you're dreaming while in a dream and then, after realizing this, being able to control what happens in the dream.
- *Dream incubation* means concentrating on a problem or question in your waking life so that a specific dream topic will occur as you sleep.

Dreams Past

Dreaming is universal. Everyone does it, yet how people regard their dreams varies dramatically from culture to culture and time period to time period. More often than not, dreaming has been associated with the divine. Let's take a brief look back. In her article "Understanding Dreams," scholar Gail Bixler-Thomas details the vivid history of dreams, starting with the earliest known record of dreams, which comes from about 5,000 years ago in Mesopotamia. And 3,700 years ago in Babylon, the *Epic of Gilgamesh,* one of the earliest known classical stories (and epic poems), reports on recurring dreams. (The hero, Gilgamesh, has dreams that inform him of the best ways to kill the monster he's after.) In the Hebrew Torah, biblical big guys such as Solomon, Jacob, and Joseph made some pretty weighty decisions based on divine guidance given in their dreams. Both the *Upanishads,* the sacred Hindu text, and the Talmud, the Jewish collection of religious writings, feature much discussion of dreams. The Talmud mentions dreams more than two hundred times, saying, for example, that dreams that are not understood are like letters that are not opened.

Bixler-Thomas informs us that in ancient Egypt, seekers of divine wisdom would incubate in temples to help ensure enlightening dreams from the dream god Serapis, often fasting, praying, or even painting or dancing to please the god and draw forth his gift. The Chinese believed that the *hun,* or spiritual soul, leaves the body and visits the land of the dead during dream time. The Chinese also had dream incubation temples, and judges and government officials were often required to visit dream temples for insight and wisdom.

96

(Imagine the Supreme Court making decisions based on revelations during pillow time. . . .)

Historically, dreams have been used by tribal shamans in native cultures to diagnose and cure both physical and psychological illnesses. The same goes for ancient Greece, where the healing god Asclepius (he of the caduceus, the staff with coiled snakes wrapped around it, which still symbolizes the medical profession today) was believed to visit sleepers in his temple and either miraculously cure them or prescribe certain herbs, spiritual practices, and exercises that would help them heal. (Sure beats sitting in a hospital room, no?) But according to Bixler-Thomas, for a period of nearly 2,000 years, from the beginning of the Christian era until Austrian psychoanalyst Sigmund Freud wrote his groundbreaking book *Die Traumdeutung* (*The Interpretation of Dreams*), dreams in the Western world were dismissed as insignificant mental masturbation and, hence, no one gave much of a damn about silly dream interpretation. Although Freud may have floated the dream boat back into popular culture again, even he believed that ultimately, dreams were delusions and manifestations of psychosis and, basically, ids gone wild.

Carl Rocks While Sigmund Rolls

Then, much to the sleepless relief of Serapis and other long-ignored dream energies, along came brilliant Swiss psychoanalyst (and Freud comrade) Carl Jung. Jung stepped straight into the dream world and shook people all night long. Whereas Freud believed that dreams were all about sex and repressed memory and disturbing stuff about how your mother treated you when you were a kid, Jung believed dreams were an untapped, powerful tool to help us heal and grow. How? Through the analysis of all the archetypal symbols and imagery that were packed into our dreams like fish in a pond.

Simply put, an archetypal symbol is a prototype, an overarching idea of some facet of human life, sent to us from the collective unconscious, which Bixler-Thomas says is the innate, inherited, universal piece of the unconscious that is believed to be the same in all people. These symbols help us recognize and integrate parts of ourselves that we have disowned or are hesitant about. Archetypes are abundant in all our common myths, fairy tales, and religions, as well as dreams. See if you've heard of a few of these: the trickster, the devil, the child, the hero, the virgin, the whore, the teacher, the magician, the sage. All of these are broad archetypes that Jung believes we share, in addition to those connected with natural objects such as the sun, moon, stars, planets, mountains, lakes, elements (earth, air, fire, water), animals, and natural cycles like life, death, and rebirth. Jung believed strongly in the power of signs, and he believed that when they come, they speak in dreams.

By the time Jung retired, Bixler-Thomas tells us, he estimated he had interpreted upwards of 80,000 dreams. He theorized that when it comes to dream imagery, we all share a universal pattern and that if we let it, this imagery can be a great facilitator of psychological, emotional, and spiritual healing. Jung was one of the first modern scientists to suggest that by observing the unique patterns and analyzing the seemingly weird symbols that pop up in our own dreams, we can actually become more self-realized, fully conscious, whole—a process Jung termed *individuation*. And what's more, during this precarious dance toward discovering (and, later, embracing) our

distinct individuality, we can overcome many personal problems, fears, and anxieties while realizing our full potential, our special purpose, our true divine spark. (And you thought your dreams were just crazy whirling mutations of funky stuff that happened to you during your day.) Jung is widely considered the first psychoanalyst to connect dreams to spirituality, and spirituality to self-development. In other words, Carl *rocks*.

Do You Individuate?

According to Jung, our conscious life is all wrapped up in the ego—our personality, quirks, habits, mental gymnastics, childhood issues—but the truth is, there are many other peripheral realities that we can more easily access in dream time. Simply put, Jung said that if you can quiet that chattering ego of yours (for instance, in sleep or through deep meditation), well, you can gain one hell of a lot more access to the mystery and magic of life and, hence, to the divine.

The brilliant Jungian teacher Penelope Rick describes Jung's process of individuation by way of this image: Imagine walking into a dark theater (your self) where a play is going on. All you can clearly see is what the spotlight (your consciousness) from above is focused on. You cannot see the chairs, the audience members, or all the other props and people and dust bunnies (your "shadow," or unconscious) that are also in the theater. The work of a lifetime, the process of individuation, is the widening of that spotlight so much that *everything* is illuminated and you are conscious of and can see your All. The theater of your self is completely ablaze with light. The conscious and the unconscious are both realized, unified, and celebrated. You are unique, individualized, yet fully in communion with the collective and with the divine. You are whole.

Now why isn't everyone shining their huge lights right and left and up and down? Why aren't we all easily illuminated? Well, for one thing, because most of us think that what's in the small spotlight *is* our All. No one has taught us differently, and only a few are helping us learn how to shine more fully. And sometimes, well, we're just lazy, or intimidated, or more than a little anxious. After all, when you expand that light in your dusky ol' theater, you may not like everything you see (which we shall address in the next chapter). The shadow part of your unconscious contains all that hasn't been allowed to fully form or develop. The shadow contains pieces of our beautiful, unrealized talents and gifts, but it's also often full of grotesque hunks of us that have not been given the attention they need, so they're sitting way off in the dank corners of our selves, withered and frightening like some hissing little horror-movie demon thing. And why the hell would anyone want to deal with that? Well, there is one cool reason: By blazing that light of true awareness down onto our fears or grimy unknown parts, we can actually release them, which frees us to be more fully ourselves.

Here's the kicker (and then I promise we'll drop this spotlight metaphor before you start yawning): You can't control your light or force it to shine wider, but you *can* invite the light in (or intend to be open to it) and be willing to bravely deal with what shows up, and shows up, and shows up. You can allow (or stop resisting) your natural divine process. I mean, really, who wants to have all those unfamiliar people and things in her theater? Who wants slimy demons hissing in her closet? Don't you want to know whether the audience members are clapping or booing or yawning or whether the props are blocking your view or helping you see clearer? Of course you do.

Where Did You Go Last Night?

You say Jungian theory doesn't inspire you? No problem. I promise, your dreams will. So how do you start interpreting them? The same way you interpret any of the other signs, symbols, or divine winks that show up in your waking life—through practice and commitment and by keeping a pen and paper (or your red book) next to your bed. Of course, there is no fixed interpretation; each dream is unique and must be approached as such and viewed from all angles. But here are some common steps that many dream experts recommend in order to amplify a dream or elaborate on it, so that you can determine its significance:

- Write the sucker down, first thing in the morning (before all the thoughts of the world rush back in) or when you wake up from a dream in the middle of the night. Write in present tense (for example, "I'm running down the beach, and there's a giant blue duck chasing me with a Vidal Sassoon curling iron"), recording all the images in the order you remember them, without editing or letting logic get in the way. Don't like writing in the middle of the night? Get a cheap digital voice recorder and record your thoughts. Listen back later, and write 'em down then.

- Pick out and underline the specific ingredients in the dream: people, places, colors, sounds, clothes, body gestures, movements, and so on.
- Next to each ingredient, write down any and all personal (direct) associations and feelings *you* have about the elements and images. How do they speak to you, both literally and symbolically? (Note: Dreams are notorious for puns; for instance, in a dream in which your sister keeps offering you her new lipstick when you're about to say something extra cutting and unnecessary to your mom, your unconscious may be offering up an idea of your *lips sticking* together, possibly hinting for you to shut your mouth concerning this issue with your mother.)
- As you go about your day, try to be aware of any cultural significance those themes and symbols might have or any similarities within religion, psychology, mythology, fairy tales, and so on. Do some research.
- You can also use what's called *active imagining*, in which you meditate or concentrate on a specific dream image and then allow your imagination to take off and see what turns up. Go ahead, free associate.
- Then think about what happened yesterday. Do any events stand out? Phone conversations? TV show themes that might have sparked something? A strange encounter on the bus?

Persistence is key. Do this for a while, and I can virtually guarantee that insights will begin to emerge, the dream meanings to shift and develop more and more. I can't tell you how many of my dreams make absolutely no sense to me at the beginning—total gobbledy-gook—but I write 'em down anyway. And sure enough, days, months, or sometimes even years later, when I re-read my journal, I am always amazed at how right on they were in reflecting what was really bubbling just beneath the surface of my life (except that really weird stuff about penguins and burlesque dancers that I still haven't quite figured out). Our unconscious and the divine are patient. If we don't understand what something means, another dream will show up, demonstrating the theme in a different way, and then another, till we jump out of bed, screaming, "Aha! I get it now! That dream about my boss, my cat, and the refrigerator with the cool Pumas probably means I'm projecting my fears of inadequacy in the workplace onto my boss and coworkers, which is causing me to stifle my creativity and go into competitive hyperdrive, which is keeping everyone I care about at a distance and my self totally malnourished! Or something like that. Whoa!"

Like a memory, just sitting there, drumming its fingers, waiting for you to recall it, the unconscious is found within all aspects of your life. Don't separate your dream life from your waking life; they are fused, interconnected and interdependent, constantly feeding each other information and energy. Jung believed that, try as you might, you can't really escape having encounters with your unconscious, because the unconscious is always striving to produce wholeness. Jung liked to quote Erasmus's observation: "Called or uncalled, God is always present."

Dreams are teachers with a slightly cryptic, mystical lesson plan. We can either learn through the dreams or have the lessons come crashing through in our waking life. For example, if you won't learn how to take pride in who you are and start using your unique gifts of creativity in your job, well, then maybe the workplace will become a more and more miserable environment to exist in, or perhaps your coworkers will become sick of you projecting on them and stop being so friendly and helpful and covering for your "sick" days, or eventually you might get fired—yikes! Bottom line: One way or another, what you need to learn in order to grow is going to pop up, and up, and up, until you finally get it and you can move on to the next layer, the next beautiful shadow that wants to become realized.

Dream Catcher

Here's a funny thing: Some people truly believe they don't dream at all. But they do. Everyone does. It's the remembering part that takes practice. A simple method for getting your mind to remember your nightly frolics in dreamland is, well, simply to ask. Seriously. Before you snore off into la la land, send out a request, either aloud or in your mind, to the divine dream energies of your world (Asclepius, by the way, would love a modern request; no one calls him directly anymore), and intend, ask to please remember your dreams, and I promise you, it'll start to happen. When it does, in the morning, try to wake up slowly, not with a jarring alarm beep. And don't wait till after you go to the bathroom or shower or brew your coffee to write down the details of the previous night's dreams; if you do, you're almost guaranteed to forget. Do it *immediately*, right after you shut off your alarm and before you leave the warm, salty confines of your bed. Studies have shown that it only takes five minutes after the end of a dream for us to forget 50 percent of the content, and ten minutes later, we've forgotten 90 percent. (The theory goes that all your dream loss is due to early-morning motor movements.) Some say that vitamin B6 can help you to remember your dreams better, too. (B6 improves mental clarity, so why not unconscious clarity?) Who knows? Just write 'em down.

≈ Dreams That Changed the World ≈

- Mary Shelley got the idea for *Frankenstein* from a slightly disturbing dream. The great Romantic poet Samuel Taylor Coleridge wrote two of his most famous works, "Rime of the Ancient Mariner" and "Kubla Khan," after waking from a fever dream. Legend has it that Coleridge began the stunning "Kubla Khan" immediately after waking up, but just as he was getting going, someone knocked on his front door and he made the terrible mistake of getting up to answer it. When he sat down again, the dream was gone.
- Paul McCartney, Billy Joel, and even Beethoven are just a few who've heard musical arrangements or lyrics while snoozin'.
- Jack Nicklaus supposedly received golf tips through his dreams.
- The prophet Muhammad (the founder of Islam) was believed to have received much of the Koran via dreams.
- Albert Einstein had an intense dream about sledding really fast down a hill at night and seeing the stars change their appearance. Pondering that dream, he developed the principle of relativity, perhaps the most famous and world-altering law in all of physics.

Leave Your Village

The Red Book believes dreams are yet another way that Spirit pokes our world to try and get our attention, so we can begin to realize who we truly are. But in order to do it, we usually have to step out of what we've always been. Jung's theory is that individuation—the difficult but totally worthwhile process of becoming whole (or holy)—begins when you leave the collective thinking of your upbringing, the safety of the flock, and embark on a path unique to your own self. Because often, it takes breaking away from the herd for you to start seeing your unique potential. No one has ever said, "I totally followed the crowd and stopped thinking for myself and let others tell me what to believe, and now I feel whole and independent." Well, OK, maybe some have said that, but, man, are *they* in for a shock.

Jung himself had powerful inner experiences, based in his process of individuation, in which he came to know his Self. (Jung developed a psychological concept that we each consist of a self we know of as our conscious personality and a self we may *not* yet fully know, one that many of us today would term our "God self"—that is; that which is us but also much bigger than us, more universal. Our conscious personality self fits within the God self, and they do a tandem dance throughout our life.) When asked, "Do you believe in God?" Jung is said to have sputtered, "I could not say I *believe*—I *know!*" Jung felt that his profound inner experiences were another face of God, but a face that was *not* very similar to the God he heard about in churches and sermons. He saw the divine as a living mystery deep in our psyches that could be (and should be) personally

Dive Deep

encountered, but he believed that one had to take the necessary journey to reach It.

That journey has been reflected in our various mythologies for as long as we've been able to tell stories: The heroine leaves her small, safe village and ventures into the dark, unknown forest alone, where she endures harsh tests of will and fortitude and has great adventures and befriends odd characters, receives special powers and gifts, encounters terrifying monsters, and usually slays or makes peace with at least one really nasty, bad-ass dragon (bravely going within and facing and accepting and thus reintegrating all parts of herself), thereby liberating herself and finding the treasure (her God self or divine spark), and so returns home triumphant and unified, fully one unto her self. It's the classic story of a life lived, a spirit fully embodied, a woman daring to be more. This is the story that each of us has inside of us, the story that each dream calls us to participate in and that each day offers, if we have the courage to dive deep within.

CHAPTER 8

Peeling Your Onion
Who Do You Think You Are?

arl Jung was right: You can't establish an authentic relationship with the divine if you don't take the time to establish an authentic relationship with yourself. In other words, there's no way you can effectively ignite your inner fire if you have no idea about who you really are. So let's start exploring you. The only real requirement for starting this process is your sincere willingness to go there. Your intent means *everything*. So right now, at this very moment, intend (again) to know your divine self—*all* of your self, not just the angelic parts. Intend to be discerning and honest and responsible with whatever you find. Intend self-love. Intend laughter and health and a strong support system, for while diving deep within can be intensely liberating and rejuvenating, it can also be disorienting, frightening, and more than a little jarring. Rest assured, you are fully capable. After all, this sort of divine self-awareness is the fundamental reason you're alive. The only question is, just how far down the rabbit hole are you willing to go?

Your Skin May Stink

Jainism, a religion from India that combines many elements of Hinduism and Buddhism, has a technique for self-realization (or coming to know your divine spark) that is sometimes likened to peeling away the layers of an onion. The practice goes like this: You ask, "Who am I?" and then answer: "I am _____" filling in the blank with something that would normally define you—for example, a stockbroker, a woman, an American, a Jew. In response to that response, you say, "I am not that!" Then you ask and respond again, and again, and again, getting ever closer to your core. The point is to keep digging, to keep looking behind and beyond your beliefs. German mystic Meister Eckhart said, "A human being has so many skins inside, covering the depths of the heart. We know so many things, but we don't know ourselves."

Igniting your divine spark is a process that *always* entails some form of "peeling your onion," and undergoing it means you must have a willingness to go below all those sticky, smelly surfaces to examine and, often, eliminate convenient titles and assumptions. It's a gentle inquiry into not only your personal beliefs but also long-held cultural, social, political, and religious ideologies. It takes time and compassion and perhaps a lot of really good chocolate. It requires you to question everything, to ask yourself, over and over again, about every aspect of your life and see how your answers begin to change.

You might ask, "Am I only a lawyer (sister, best friend, lover, despiser of small yappy dogs)? Or is who I really am not contingent on those labels?" You might say, "Do I *really* believe I have to be thin (voluptuous), married (single), a CEO (starving artist), a quiet (loud), demure (demanding), saintly (beastly) spiritual paragon (atheist) in order to matter or to make myself feel alive or valid? If so (or if not), where did this belief come from? My mom? My teacher? That book? My church, my social circle, that magazine?"

Once you've asked about titles and labels, you begin to ask about function. In other words, you may now want to ask, "How

III

does this belief or label serve me? Does it keep me healthy? Does it keep me safe? Does it make me more loving and compassionate and grateful? Or does it keep me closed, dependent on external opinion, afraid to stand up on my own? Does it invite new experiences into my life, new ways of viewing my reality, new relationships? Does it limit my perspective or enhance it? Does it help me express my full potential? Does it authentically empower me?" And so on.

So, as a regular practice, keep asking yourself questions, from the simple to the complex, the sacred to the profane, the serious to the silly. Here are a few more starter questions, which may or may not apply to you. Please feel free to whip out your red book and write down a few hundred more of your own, but start asking.

- What really scares me, and why?
- What sort of people do I attract into my life?
- Do I fear change? Do I fear staying the same?
- Do I ignore my intuition? Do I even have any idea what it is?
- Do I shove my true feelings down?
- Do I fear my own power? Do I misuse what power I have?
- Am I sexually honest and following my body's true needs?
- Is that food/drug/drink really what my body needs right now? What am I truly hungry for?
- Does this job sustain me on all levels?
- Why do I always get sick on family holidays when I have to go home for a visit?
- Why am I so judgmental about my sister, myself—shit, everyone?
- Why does questioning myself make me want to run for the hills with some aspirin and a really good bottle of tequila?

This is your personal territory, so create your own questions. After you've written down the questions, go ahead and try to write down the answers. Or better yet, sing them out in the shower, so you can wash your old perceptions of yourself down the drain. (This may sound silly, but believe me, on an energetic level, such metaphors and visualizations truly help.) Don't overanalyze or think you must book an appointment with your therapist for the next hundred Wednesdays. Sometimes just noticing your patterns is enough. And please, don't try to answer all your questions at once. Just sit with them. Perhaps meditate on one per week, or even one per month. Remember: onion. It's a continuous process; there are always skins to shed, new layers to slough off, new aspects of self to realize. You might get one answer to your question one day, another the next month, and even another the next decade. It is not meant to be instant, nor is it meant to solve everything. It is, like everything else, merely part of the revelatory, ongoing process.

After all, we are *always* becoming more of who we are. The story is never complete, the painting is never finished, the great tree of your spirit never stops growing and branching out and digging its roots deeper and deeper into the soil of meaning. Spiritual writer LaSara FireFox says, in her awesome book *Sexy Witch,* that we are *constantly* self-defining, which is the means to self-determination, which is the ability to make your own choices, unconstrained by the thoughts or illusions of others or by the culture in which you live. As the great American poet E. E. Cummings (1884–1962) said, "To be nobody-but-yourself—in a world which is doing its best, night and day, to make you everybody else—means to fight the hardest battle which any human being can fight; and never stop fighting."

113

This is when the fun really begins. Because when you start to go below your surfaces, when you not only begin to shed all those rules and labels that ostensibly tell you who and what you are but also are willing to look at your ego up close and personal, aspects of yourself that you never knew existed or that you purposefully shoved away (remember Jung's shadow?) will suddenly emerge and demand attention. When you are learning how to master yourself, fears, vices, unhealthy tendencies, and your secret obsession with *The Bachelor* all might come up for a square-off. But in the midst of these will arise astounding and bedazzling notions of your natural beauty, your divine purpose, your healthy desires, your heart's beat, and most important, a refreshed sense of personal freedom.

Strip Teasing Your Self

Many of us start realizing who we are by realizing who we are not. And once we see who we are not, we sometimes need to get rid of the notions that reinforce the old ideas of who we are. (Here's where performing meaningful "releasing" rituals always helps.) As German political journalist Ludwig Börne (1786–1832) wisely said, "Losing an illusion makes you wiser than finding a truth." Self-realization is about letting go of that which no longer serves your highest potential—for example, by ending unhealthy relationships, burning old journals, cleaning out your closets, or nixing your inner critic—so you can start to see, attract, and use what does serve your highest self. This is a very brave way to move through life; often, it's extremely difficult to say good-bye to people, places, jobs, things, habits, foods, and beliefs that, up to now, have defined who you are and kept you, well, "you." By letting go of what no longer serves us, we are making more room for what serves us much, much better.

So let's say you intuit, perhaps through emotions, physical sensations, divine signs, dreams, or meditations, that your job or sour boyfriend or harsh diet or everyday stiletto traipsing might not be so healthy for you anymore. Trust yourself. Don't let voices of doubt and self-deception immediately jump back in (they will always try); trust that your intuitive guidance is present, not to force unnecessary change on you that will make you miserable but to ultimately make you more than you could ever have imagined. Trust that your spirit wants you ultimately to have a sexually delicious, happy, and empowering relationship; a financially secure and personally rewarding career; and healthy eating habits, preferably all while wearing amazingly adorable yet perhaps more spine-supportive shoes. (Seriously, about the shoes.) So your inner self is asking you to make some choices and make some changes that will allow all that yummy goodness to come seeping into your immediate reality.

And remember, it's not always about the choice you make but, rather, the reasons *behind* the choice. Why are you staying in that strained relationship? Because you truly love this person and realize that your desire to flee is just another flare-up of your nasty habit of avoiding your intimacy issues? Or are you sticking around because you're scared, scared to be alone and scared you won't find a new love, and because you're, in fact, co-dependent? Be open to hearing your truth, even if it hurts.

Mind F✳ck

Most of us, when faced with a powerfully intuitive notion, will let the brain rush in and overpower it, analyze everything, and try to think through the issue instead of letting that sometimes vague, "weaker" intuitive feeling guide our actions. We all do it, and we all know how often that approach seems to fall far short of fulfilling our needs or solving the problem.

Simply put, you can't always figure out what needs to change by just sitting and thinking it through, trying to force-fit it all together in your head using pure reason and cold logic. Because as wonderful as our minds are, when it comes to making important shifts, they can sometimes be tricky little suckers who confuse the hell out of us. Like when we get the feeling that it might be time to get rid of those clothes we don't wear anymore and that remind us of that nail-bitingly painful relationship, but then our mind starts shooting us full of thoughts like "Those clothes are really pretty, and you might need them later for some future event or if that style comes back in, and then you'll totally regret this, and what if you're just intuiting wrong or just reactive and bored and really just needing more, more, more—I know, let's go shopping!" And then, there you are, two years later, stuck with the same damn pile, now surrounded by a whole bunch of other piles. This is the problem with the ego (whose favorite habitat is the mind). It has a hard time letting go and can think of a million reasons why you shouldn't. But when it comes to your divine spark (which communicates via intuitions), there is no guesswork, no analysis, no million possible alternatives. Your spirit just *knows*.

☞ The Body Barometer ☜

I can't tell you how many times I've known, from my deepest self, that I needed to move on or make an uncomfortable change, but fear kept me scared stiff. It happens to all of us. I reacted to my intuition the way many of us do: I hoped the vibes would go away and leave me the hell alone. Not a good idea. Every time I did this, without fail, my body would start to act up—migraines, irritable bowel, sinus infections, eczema, horrible menstrual periods, you name it. The fact is, my body wasn't going to just sit by and let me deny my truth. Now, I'm not saying every illness or rash or stomachache is due to you ignoring your truth, but for me and for several other people I know, when we disregard the deep knowledge that change is wanted in our life, sooner or later, the body will let us know—and not in a good way.

The body never lies. It's your spiritual tuning fork. So it's your responsibility not to merely cover up its signals with expensive lotions and Pepto-Bismol but to sit down and really *listen* to what is underneath those symptoms.

But while your intuition might not ever say the wrong thing, it sometimes *can* be difficult to discern from your ego. So if you're not quite sure that what you're sensing you need to change or let go of is really right or timely, ask the universe to give you some clearer signs. Get quiet and meditate on it. Perhaps ask for support from a trusted teacher, family member, or friend.

Oh, but there are always things that jump in our way that maybe don't even mean to do so but just can't seem to help it. Sometimes our loved ones or our teachers don't want us to change, not because they don't love us but because if we change, our relationships with them might change. We will still be a loving daughter (friend, lover, student), but we might not let them cross our boundaries as much, might not need as much emotional coddling, might not depend on them anymore to mentor us and give us all the answers (which makes them feel important). In short, we might start seeing them differently, a notion that can make just about anyone uncomfortable. Furthermore, when we begin to live from our true self (that is, from our truth), sometimes those close to us feel suddenly very self-conscious and awkward, not because our opinions of them have changed but because living our truth reveals the areas in which *they* might not be living from *their* truth. That said, more often than not, during particularly intense times of change and inner turmoil, I've received the most absolutely perfect advice and openly loving support from someone close to me. Which response can you expect from those close to you? It's impossible to say, until you begin.

≈ You Talkin' to Me? ≈

Countless spiritual traditions treat the ego like a rabid monkey with a severe personality disorder—something that desperately needs to be shut away or even put out of its misery. But the truth is, we need our ego in order to take care of our basic survival needs (food, shelter, physical safety) so that our divine spark can blaze more freely. The problem is, most of us let the ego's overly protective voice override the voice of our fun-loving spirit. As the saying goes, the ego is a lousy master, but an excellent servant. In her wonderfully helpful article "Spirit Versus Ego," author and life coach Mary Allen gives a few hints on how to figure out which of the two forces is taking the lead in your life. Allen says the spirit's "voice" is more free, creative, playful, and warm, whereas the ego speaks more practically, cautiously, protectively, and judgmentally. The ego blames, criticizes, compares, and makes excuses (sound familiar?). Its favorite word is *should* (hey, quit shoulding all over yourself). The ego fears getting hurt, wants to remain safe, and is always worried about what other people think. What's more, the ego looks for answers almost solely from the mind, rarely from the heart. Too much reliance on the ego keeps you separate from the spiritual nature of the world, from others, from your true power. When it kicks into overdrive, ego can manifest as separation, resistance, victimization, confusion, restriction, suppression, stress, fear, and shame. On the flip side, when spirit rules, it's all about love, nurturing, openness, trust, acceptance, courage, connection, heart, responsibility, inspiration, and peace. Quite a difference, no?

So if you get a nudge to shift your life around or you are reacting to change in a particular way, check to see if you are coming from your ego or your spirit. See which of the preceding terms apply to your situation. If it's your ego, give it a metaphorical vodka martini and the night off.

Just a quick reminder to not go all puritanical on yourself. You don't need to take peeling the onion and self-cleansing so far that you end up living alone in the woods dressed in dried bark and hemp, never to wear your Manolos again because they don't serve your highest potential. Remember, don't do anything, or get rid of anything, or take on anything just because you think it makes you "more spiritual" or because it's what "spiritual" people do. Do it because it's true to what you are sensing is needed in your life at this particular time. Know that ultimately, the decision to make waves in your life must come from deep inside you in order to have the desired soul-shining effect.

Accept Your Self

This seems like a good time to introduce a small paradox: While it's vital to make appropriate change in your life when your divine spark nudges you to, it's often even *more* important to accept and (gulp) even learn to love where you are right now. In fact, acceptance of our current situation often needs to come before we can truly move forward.

It's tough to totally accept yourself as perfect and divinely becoming even when you just tripped and fell down the stairs at your high school reunion or when you screamed those horribly biting words at your significant other or when you forgot to feed your cat, again. How about when you realize that you snap at your best friend not because her seemingly endless dramatics annoy the hell out of you but because deep down you have never liked or been able to accept your own inner drama queen? Or how about when you're

exploring your inner self and, yikes, you see how much deep anger you hold toward humanity, life, yourself? Can you accept yourself, knowing how manipulative you can be or how your apparent shyness and lack of confidence is not really about being humble but is actually a form of arrogance, because when you play small, you are, in essence, denying the divine's grandness? Accepting and loving who you are without judgment, without constantly measuring faults and supposed flaws, can be a formidable challenge, but it can also help generate the necessary energy for authentic change. If we're busy condemning or avoiding our issues or are busy denying who we are right now, we're at war with our reality, we're not being truthful or living in the present moment, and we're not able to rest at the only place inside us from which we can truly spring forward.

Spiritual teacher Jack Kornfield writes, in his wonderful book *A Path with Heart:* "Much of spiritual life is self acceptance, maybe all of it" (p. 47). In other words, maybe enlightenment isn't some grand, elevated state of blissful transcendental ecstasy but, rather, a calm and peaceful and loving inner knowing of who we are and accepting what is. Spiritual teacher Marianne Williamson says, in her lectures based on the spiritually complex book *A Course in Miracles,* that all the divine is, is the love inside you. To have a relationship with the divine is to have a relationship with the love inside you. So letting the divine love you is the same thing as loving yourself, and loving your self is the same as loving the divine. Get it?

When we start journeying inward and seeing all the diamonds and poisons, balms and knives we've got stored away, it's imperative that we tread lightly and flood what we find with a sense of love and compassion. It's not enough to merely acknowledge that you might have some demons; you've got to learn how to wholeheartedly accept their existence so you can eventually smooch 'em to death. As Walt Whitman so famously said in his epic poem *Song of Myself,* "Not an inch nor a particle of an inch is vile, and none shall be less familiar than the rest" (p. 27). It's crucial that we practice unconditional love for ourselves, for it's in these kinds of tender, heart-opening moments that we best emulate the divine. It is here that we realize that there is nothing, absolutely nothing in us that is not trying to grow into love.

You Cannot Force a Rose to Bloom

So please, take it easy on yourself. As with anything, you can go overboard with spiritual work and get too caught up in your particular process and method of onion peeling. Igniting your divine spark *does* require passionate intent, it can be hard work, and it will effect change, but that doesn't mean you have to *force* it. This is not some sort of popularity contest for the soul, a race to some indefinable level of enlightenment. Divinity is always on time. Your time.

That's right, sometimes we change almost by accident. We can't help it. Sometimes just by opening up, just by actively intending to sink deeper into your existence, things that no longer fit in your life begin to fall away. Naturally. Softly. Almost unnoticeably. Nothing is resisted; instead, everything is allowed. In this resting place, spirituality becomes less about doing and more about simply being.

Remember to kick back once in a while, lighten up, shove all this away, and give your self a gentle squeeze. A regular splash of humor, friends, your favorite music, long walks, and whatever else

≈ Take A Load Off ≈

Beware of any belief, teacher, practice, or tradition that makes you feel like you have to do *so* much or become something or someone *so* different in order to be self-realized or enlightened. Likewise, beware of those who tell you that there is some perfect ultimate enlightened state you're supposed to reach, eventually, if you meditate enough or listen to your intuition absolutely, or drink enough grape Kool-Aid. Notions of self-realization, when taken out of context or abused, can make you feel like you are innately lacking something, that you are separate from and not (yet) divine, here and now. Such distortions do not help you learn how to trust your unique and organic process. This can be extremely disheartening or induce panic and fear. And that is no good. Spirituality offers many ways for us to remember and reconnect with our innate divine spark, many of which do inspire personal change. But spirituality should never, ever make you feel less than divine for being who you are now.

helps you live in love will help keep you sane and balanced during this wobbly and uncharted process. But all the same, no matter how in or out of balance you may become at times, it's OK. We are not here to be perfect. Don't take yourself too seriously or your shadows too personally. It is actually quite simple, despite its apparent complexity. Know thyself, then be thyself. And of course, love thyself. And that's all She wrote.

CHAPTER 9

When Sparks Fly
Know Your Self,
Transform the World

We now interrupt this program for a word from one of our deliciously red sponsors: the Gnostics. *The Red Book* has been talking an awful lot about how to know yourself is to know the divine, but let's pause for a moment to ground this seemingly New Age-y idea deep in some extraordinary religious history, and give ourselves some healthy reminders.

Maybe you've heard of the Gnostic gospels? Novelist Dan Brown referred to these famous "lost" holy scriptures frequently in his huge (and controversial) bestseller *The Da Vinci Code,* and Carl Jung was heavily influenced by their teachings, too. Simply put, the Gnostic gospels are a collection of remarkable teachings that were written by Jesus' disciples but viewed as dangerous and heretical by the early (second century C.E.) church fathers and therefore banned from the official Christian canon. In fact, the whole spiritual tradition that rose up around these teachings, called *Gnosticism,* from the Greek word *gnosis,* meaning "inner knowing" and "self-knowledge," was outlawed by the early Church; the church leaders even went so far as to attempt to destroy the gospels. Lucky for us (and history), some cunning followers managed to hide them away and keep them secret for centuries. No one knew what became of them until 1945, when they were found buried in a clay pot in the desert near the town of Nag Hammadi in Egypt. (Yet another way that heaven has said "Boo!")

So just what sort of radical, heretical beliefs do these famous texts contain? Why such a vicious effort to destroy them? Well, Lance S. Owens, in his article "An Introduction to Gnosticism and the Nag Hammadi Library," says that the Gnostics were a big problem for the Church because they very much believed that a direct, personal, absolute knowing of ultimate truth is accessible to *all* human beings, a knowing that follows no logical or rational understanding but is acquired by way of—you guessed it—personal experience. Strict religious dogma was to the Gnostics what a bicycle is to a fish: a useless unidirectional contraption. For them, *ongoing divine revelation* was what it was all about. If you were a Gnostic, you accessed this type of sacred revelation *not* by going outside, not by listening solely to others or by reading theology or by being dictated to but by looking *inside* and finding your deep inner self, your "self of your self," which was often referred to as a divine seed or a divine spark and which was believed to be the *same substance as God.* This experience of one's divine spark was a human being's truest reality, and it was cause for celebration by humans *and* the divine. You know, Jesus always said the kingdom of God is *within* you, so—maybe he was more of a Gnostic than the church fathers led us to believe.

Owens goes on to say that according to Gnosticism, if you came to know your inner spark, you would understand that you are truly free, that you are not sinful or blemished flesh separated from God but are actually the *very stuff* of the divine and a *conduit* of the divine's immanent realization. Scholar Elaine Pagels, author of *The Gnostic Gospels,* has said that the secret of Gnosticism is this: To know your deep self is to simultaneously know God. ("Preposterous!" the early church fathers wail, as they spin in their graves.) Sure enough, it's the sort of idea that would have completely upstaged and up-ended the early Church; after all, who would need a dogmatic religious father figure if people realized they already *had* the divine within and required no stern intermediaries (though compassionate guidance and support is always helpful) to access it? They could find out what God was, just by checking *in*. Carl Jung believed that "one of the main functions of organized religion is to protect people from a direct experience of God." I don't know whether he was entirely right, but I can't help but wonder where we as a culture, as a world, would be now if the Gnostic version of intuitive, exper-iential spiritual knowing had been allowed to blossom in the main-stream. Imagine *that* possibility for a while—unless it makes you all depressed and bitter, in which case just laugh and sigh and thank the Goddess that enlightening information like this is now as common as a cold. Anyone can catch it. Hey, you just did.

Believe Me, You Need to Know You

As the Gnostics well knew, there is a difference between intellectually *believing* you are divine ("hey cool, I'm divine!") and truly *knowing* you are divine through direct, conscious experience ("holy shit! I AM Divine!"). It's a bit like the difference between believing in the *idea* of eating healthier—as in, you read a lot about it, and your health-nut friends all tell you it works and you tell your dad to do it, and you

occasionally swap sausage for tofu—and actually having the energized, personal experience of glowing physical health because you have consciously changed your *own* diet. It's not just about reading the diet articles in *Self* and stuffing yourself with organic broccoli and brown rice; it's about truly *feeling the difference,* deep down, and realizing your own fundamental power to affect your body, your health, and, hence, your spirit. See the distinction? There's a key transition between intellectual awareness and lived reality. A similar shift happens when you move from *thinking* you're divine to *knowing* you're divine.

Yep, here it is, perhaps the best part about exploring spirituality: No matter what I write in this book or what fabulous information and wisdom you learn from the Gnostics or that teacher, class, or bus ride, none of it really matters, none of it will truly hit home until you directly experience these beliefs yourself, until your beliefs are translated into deep-down, cell-level *knowing.* There is simply no way for me to tell you, no way for me to know what will flip that switch in you, what event or word or wink or orgasm or book or dream or meditation or prayer or divine burrito will cause that essential shift, but I can promise you one thing: If you keep yourself open, ready, and primed, at some point, you *will* know. The shift will happen. Perhaps it already has. For most of us, it's an ongoing practice; some days, we truly feel it and know our divinity, and other days, that feeling couldn't be further away, and we simply have to rely on believing in it. I know, not a simply answer. Hey, this is spirituality; it's *supposed* to be a little slippery.

FLIP THAT SWITCH

Get Over Your Self

Why all this emphasis on understanding the difference between believing and knowing? Because while belief often opens the door to experience—that is, it's often the first step *toward* that deeper knowing—it's still only a limited form of the ultimate truth and can easily be misunderstood and even abused. If we're not careful, the ego can go hog-wild, jumping all over the idea of looking to our inner selves to find God and using belief as some sort of narcissistic trump card ("Hey, I believe I'm divine; I'm pretty darn special, and I believe I heard God say I can do whatever I want to whomever I please!").

How to know if you're becoming too narcissistic? Too wrapped up in the belief itself while ignoring the deeper experience that the belief is supposed to lead to? Well, generally speaking, if you have become obsessed with *your* truth, *your* path, and you *only* listen to your inner guidance and ignore the importance of ethics, community, and relationship, you probably need to step away from the spiritual mirror for a while—or just shatter it altogether and try some other approach. In my experience, if you hold strongly to your intent to know your true divine self, keep yourself open to divine signs and wise teachers, have some common sense and some well-meaning loved ones who aren't afraid to smack you over the head once in a while and give it to you straight when you've become too damn full of your divine self, you won't fall too deep into the "it's all about me, me, me" hole.

Look. Every spiritual approach has a shadow side. When you dig deep, sometimes you forget to come up for air. It's sort of inevitable. You'll have selfish periods. You'll get caught up in your

⇒ It's All About Me ⇒

When I've become too enamored with what I see in my spiritual mirror, way too caught up in thinking that my own internal process is the be-all, end-all, invariably something will wake me up. Such as bird poop—landing directly on my head. (Remember symbolic sight? Use it for *everything* in your life.) It might be a friend pointedly asking for my help with *her* illness, which means I have to get out of my own selfish head. Or I'll read or hear or see something that totally upstages my own little self-centered world. (Oprah's humanitarian aid shows often provide a good slap of perspective.) My myopic vision opens up to the larger world, and my attention to life, my self, the divine becomes more balanced.

And if those mild pinches don't work, sure enough, something bigger and more aggressive will swing at me, some undeniable wake-up call from the universe, until I finally get it. But trust me, you don't want to suffer the big reminders. They can be a real bitch. My rule: Pay attention to the little stuff, the unexpected jabs. They're probably trying to tell you something.

own internal theater. Hey, you're human. Most of us learn how to avoid staring too much into our own spiritual mirror by, well, experiencing what happens when we stare too much into our spiritual mirror. As William Blake said in his Proverbs of Hell, "You never know what is enough unless you know what is more than enough."

It's *all* part of the divine process. It *all* has the potential to show us our own divinity, eventually. The good news is, once you do start experiencing your divine spark, even a teeny-weeny bit, selfish tendencies will start to feel extremely uncomfortable, because you'll be unfolding more and more from your natural self. And your true self only knows how to move through this world in a way that is the exact opposite of narcissism. In his article "A Gnostic Worldview: A Brief Summary of Gnosticism," Stephen A. Hoeller says that inner integrity comes forth from the illumination of the indwelling spark. Gnosticism (which, by the way, many still practice today) encourages nonattachment and nonconformity, a lack of egotism and a respect for the dignity and freedom of all beings. But it's up to the intuition and wisdom of every individual (the knowing of each one's heart) to distill from these principles individual guidelines for their personal application.

➤ Free to Be Me Means Free to Be You ➤

Ever heard of a bodhisattva? In Buddhism, a bodhisattva is someone who's attained full enlightenment, who's ready and able to transcend this earthly plane at will but who's chosen to stick around this crazy, messy planet to help ease the suffering of everyone else. In fact, many bodhisattvas vow not to check out until *everyone* on this planet or even in this universe is enlightened, awake, aware of All they truly are. And living it honestly, selflessly, in a uniquely personal way that causes no harm to others. Yep, it's a big job. Those bodhisattvas have their work cut out for them. But the best part is, you don't have to be an enlightened master to help others in this kind of profound bodhisattva-like way.

Many normal, not-yet-enlightened people (like you and me) take the bodhisattva vow, which simply means that they promise to strive to become divinely conscious, not just for themselves but, more important, to help others. These Buddhas-in-the-making understand that the more they increase their own divine clarity, the more the total clarity of the world will increase. Often, of course, a person has to focus on his or her self for a bit in order to become more effective at making positive change in the external world. So, as self-focused and egotistical as our spiritual approach may seem at first ("I can't hang out, I'm busy burning off karma!" "Don't bother me with your issues, I'm trying to find my own damn self!" "Look Ma, I can breathe out of my third eye!"), it's sometimes a necessary part of the process, so that one day soon, we can truly embody that bodhisattva energy and, as Mahatma Gandhi so profoundly stated, *be* the change we wish to see in the world.

Come Up FOR AIR

It's a simple notion: The more you start experiencing the divine spark inside you, which is a deep unconditional love, the more you start experiencing the divine, the love, in *every living thing*. You realize that although we all have different relationships to and expressions of it, the divine spark is the same within each and every one of us, and as you progress, you can't help but feel how your self is connected to the whole. You become increasingly conscious that you're not so separate from the world after all. Then an amazing thing happens: Those formerly distant, detached issues like racism, prejudice, environmental devastation, social injustice, poverty, repression—anything that harms the integrity, the divine spark of humans, animals, and this planet—becomes *really* not OK with you anymore. You don't just *believe* that those things aren't right because your parents brought you up well and you have politically correct friends, you actually *feel* it in your body, your heart, your soul. Actually, you can't *not* feel it. You begin to feel, as Martin Luther King Jr. did, that "injustice anywhere is a threat to justice everywhere."

This feeling, this knowing that All is One transmutes into personal acts of service for humanity, animals, and the planet. But oneness does not mean sameness, and so such acts of service may be public and large, or quiet and seemingly small. Noah Levine, Buddhist teacher and author of *Dharma Punx,* says that after a while, the natural expression for going inward becomes, well, going outward. Ultimately, we find that our personal divine spark becomes quite *im*personal, broadcasting universal messages: "Please, be compassionate. Be of service to others. Be peaceful. Be in Love. Be alive. Be honest. Be your self. And please, don't forget to enjoy Me."

CHAPTER 10

Breaking the Rules

Healthy Transgressions Make the Heavens Applaud

Sometimes we just need to transgress. To break the rules, cross boundaries, step over restrictive lines. Here's where *The Red Book* shamelessly appropriates the Hindu Tantric concept of transgression, the notion of intentionally and mindfully cutting through social and personal norms—the cultural status quo, rules, personal patterns, behaviors—to get closer to divinity and, hence, to oneself.

Tantric practitioners, especially those of the "left-hand" variety (that is, the more esoteric and unorthodox of the two main types of Tantra) believe that by intentionally acting against the grain of social or religious mores, they jump-start their spiritual connection and access a more personal and direct union with Ultimate Reality. In India, these transgressions take the form of eating fish, meat, ingesting a particular (sometimes hallucinatory) grain, having ritualized sexual intercourse, and drinking alcohol—practices that make the right-hand practitioners squirm and recoil. But in the left-hand form of Tantra, it's believed that one must cut through perceptions of what is clean/unclean, safe/dangerous, sacred/profane in order to get close to the divine.

And so it is with you. Tantric tradition, as well as my own experience, suggests that we as young women must regularly and intentionally step outside of ourselves, out of the patterns we have settled into, in order to open new doors of perception and re-spark our connection to divinity. Transgress to break out of your mold.

Transgress to shave off the stale crusts of your life. Transgress to reinvigorate your soul's health. When you do something outside of your norm, you access another part of you that you probably didn't know (or just forgot) existed. It's fresh and flirty. In this place, you have a beginner's mind, allowing you to enjoy an experience unfettered by typical expectations, and are therefore more open to divine touchdowns.

Breaking Your Own Traditions

So what could be considered transgressive for a young woman in this day and age, learning and loving in the land of the free and already indulging in many of the left-handed Tantrika's supposedly naughty transgressions on a regular basis? Look at your life, and observe your most common patterns and habits and definitions. Maybe transgression, for you, simply means not always following the latest fashion trends, turning off the major media and exploring alternative sources, or getting rid of your TV altogether. Maybe it's dyeing your hair red or even cutting it all off, just for the hell of it, to see what happens, what new energies open up, how your world reacts. Maybe it's listening more and talking less, or speaking more clearly instead of muttering, or quitting that "great" job that has the terrific benefits and kick-ass salary but gives you no real sense of purpose.

Or maybe your transgression is not having a third drink at your best friend's birthday party, when you normally drink a bit too aggressively. Or maybe it's about letting go of your constant need to be in total control and cutting loose on your summer vacation. Maybe it's having sex outdoors, or maybe it's becoming temporarily

BREAK ALL THE RULES

137

celibate so that you can focus on healing some personal and relationship issues. Maybe it's finally trying to get that short story published, traveling to a foreign country alone, skipping mass and trying temple, skipping religion and trying nature, or belting out some karaoke when your voice can shatter glass. It could be a new route for your walk to work or a new recipe for making dinner or a wild plan to redecorate your apartment.

Let me remind you that all transgressions don't have to be visible, external acts. Try transgressing, also, against your normal thought patterns, your typical emotional responses and judgments. Can you learn to talk to yourself in a more positive way when you look in the mirror, find a more peaceful way of channeling your anger when you are fighting with your partner, or learn to gracefully accept your roommate's exuberant love affair with all things plaid? These are all internal transgressions. At this level, transgression means just about anything that incites energy for change and lifts you out of your normal routines and plops you down somewhere else, somewhere new and refreshing and pregnant with possibility.

It may not feel like repainting your bedroom a shocking new color, or turning off your TV and taking a walk (for a change), or speaking explicitly and openly for the first time with a lover have much to do with your inner path, but such simple transgressions are indeed very much a part of your spiritual practice. What's more, I encourage you to take this a step further by transgressing against your long-standing thoughts and beliefs about religion and spirituality and (yikes!) even the divine. That's right, go ahead and transgress against what you think your path "should" be if you are going to follow that leader or that doctrine or that organization or even this book (well, maybe wait until you've read a little more; there's some great stuff to come). Try transgressing against what "they" told you about God, about heaven, about karma and sin or what you need to do in order to be a good spiritual girl. Test the waters. Create your own crazy swan dive to take you deep. Dare to have a divine inner child who speaks with a pierced tongue.

Do any of the transgressions listed earlier in this chapter speak to you? The examples are plentiful, but your transgressions need to fit your unique life. After all, one woman's transgression is another's no big whoop. Examine your life, note (or, better yet, write a list of) some of your own die-hard patterns and behaviors, and then ask yourself, "What would happen if I were to suddenly do the exact opposite? What would happen if I shocked everyone I knew, including myself, and did something totally unexpected, different, unorthodox?" Now, pay attention to how you feel when you imagine these scenarios. Does merely imagining it make you nervous? A bit scared? Excited? If so, you've hit it: That behavior is ripe for transgression. In the words of philosopher Friedrich Nietzsche: "Believe me, the secret for harvesting from existence the greatest fruitfulness and greatest enjoyment is—to live dangerously" (*The Gay Science,* p. 161).

But remember, transgression is a *healthy* rebellion; it has an expansive intent. You do not need, for example, to go have random sex with a sleazy stranger just because you wouldn't normally do it. This ain't some mindless spiritual slumber-party version of truth or dare. Use your head, and see what actions or inner changes truly resonate with you. This is not an ego trip or a test of willpower,

≈ But Mom, Jesus Did It Too ≈

Eastern Tantra is not the only tradition in which transgression is encouraged. Oh no, the West has to fess up and claim one of the most transgressive rebels in history. That would be the big JC, Jesus Christ himself (well, the *historical* Jesus, anyway, not necessarily the one taught by so many faiths). Scholars have said that one of the ways they can determine whether they are reading about the real Jesus in their ancient materials is by noticing whether the words and actions in question are at odds with first-century Palestine's cultural and religious norms. He was that kind of rebel.

In his brilliant book *The Serpent's Gift: Gnostic Reflections on the Study of Religion,* Jeffrey Kripal, a professor of religious studies at Rice University, informs us that Jesus was pretty darn feisty, if not downright radical, for his day and age. Jesus frequently broke the ultra-rigid Jewish laws of purity; his disciples were told to metaphorically eat his flesh and drink his blood, he hung out with socially unsavory characters, he could always be found teaching and healing on the Sabbath, and he had some pretty interesting opinions about the sexually deviant. Kripal notes that after studying the New Testament from a historical perspective, it's nearly impossible *not* to come away with the feeling that Jesus transgressed quite on purpose, as if he were consciously *trying* to offend the religious authorities, scandalize the good and holy, and stick it to the law. So there you go. Jesus Christ, a religious anarchist. As Jung oh so controversially once said, according to Rob Brezsny in his book, *Pronoia*: "The whole point of Jesus' life was not that we should become exactly like him, but that we should become ourselves in the same way he became himself. Jesus was not the great exception but the great example" (p. 249).

designed merely to see how hard you can push yourself. Transgression is not merely to provoke or draw attention, nor is it something that should cause you or anyone else serious harm.

Transgression is not always easy, but it is a powerful method for jolting yourself out of an old perspective and into a new consciousness, giving you the chance to free up your own internal authority. You are learning how to tune into something profound—your divine self and its innocent desire to creatively express its all. And hey, by being an original you, an individual of personal and spiritual integrity, you are already transgressing most cultural and social and even religious norms. By doing something or being someone that is more you and less "them," you are teaching the world through example how to genuinely live, how to waltz through this whole charade with eyes wide open, how to be a brave woman who's not afraid to wear red to a funeral—in short, how to be truly free.

CHAPTER 11

Open Up and Say Ahhh
Sex. Spirit. The Twain Shall Meet—Under Your Covers

Ah, yes. And then there's sex. Do spiritual tools come any more potent, transgressive, and misunderstood than this? Here's the one thing you need to know, above all: Contrary to traditional belief, sex and sexuality should *not* be estranged from your spiritual practice or awareness, locked away like some guilty secret and only brought out after a few glasses of wine. As Tantrists and mystics have been declaring for centuries, sex, with the right awareness and intention, is actually an incredibly valuable and wonderfully powerful tool for spiritual growth.

Let's slip into something a little more comfortable for a moment. Ask yourself this: What feelings flood over you when you're having *really* incredible, mind-blowing sex? Ecstasy? Total bliss? How about some intense physical and emotional power? A feeling of deep connection? Or is it sort of an out-of-body meltdown, especially during orgasm? Do you feel so *connected to the present moment* that you lose all sense of space and time and bed sheets? Is there an "Oh my God!" exclamation point thrown out to the universe every once and a while? Well now, interestingly enough, that all sounds very similar to how thousands, even millions of people across history have described their most powerful and numinous spiritual experiences. In fact, the similarities are so great that many researchers now say that the ordinary act of lovemaking can be just as viable a path to higher states of consciousness, to a connection with All That Is, as meditation or prayer or any other traditional religious or spiritual ritual. How great is that?

Dr. Jenny Wade, a researcher in consciousness studies and author of the intriguing book *Transcendent Sex,* has found that ordinary people in all sorts of sexual relationships (one-night stands, monogamous, single, married, same-sex, you name it) have experienced transcendent sex—that is, sex in which their ordinary reality changed so much during lovemaking that they sometimes experienced visions or felt waves of energy and light pouring through their body. Some even traveled to other dimensions, saw deities and other spirits (uh, where did my boyfriend go?), dissolved into the Void or felt God, or had other funky experiences. Usually these experiences happen to just one of the partners, but sometimes it happens to both.

To which you might reply, oh sure, crazy visions and astral travel and whatever—sounds cool, but isn't that for those Tantric or Taoist sex people, the ones who sit cross-legged for hours and imagine their orgasms moving up their spine? Not exactly. According to Wade's research, these responses just sort of *happened* to normal people just like you, without really trying, without years of practicing esoteric techniques, and regardless of the lovers' spiritual beliefs. Wade found that the experience was often powerful enough to forever transform and enrich her subjects' lives.

Know who else sometimes gets a sexual buzz from divine interaction? Celibate nuns. It's true. In a study conducted by the Department of Psychology at the University of Montreal, Carmelite nuns (nuns who rarely leave their monastery and live a pretty austere life of silent prayer almost completely separate from the modern world) were hooked up to neuroscientific machines for EEGs and PET scans. Researchers then asked these nuns, most of whom were in their seventies or eighties, to close their eyes and try to remember (or relive) their *unio mystica* (mystical union), a religious experience that most of them had in their late twenties—a profound episode that was so intense that many claimed to sense God as an actual *physical presence*. Although you can't force a mystical experience, the neuroscientists were banking on the fact that the same parts of the brain are activated by a memory of an experience. They were right. The machines picked up brain activity in the regions previously associated with relaxation and deep meditative states. In addition, some of the nuns' *physical experiences* were noted. They characterized their *unio mystica* as bringing intense bliss, a sense of fullness (tingles, blushing, physical sensations that many would describe as sexual), and a precious sense of intimacy that forever changed their relationship with the divine. They were, to put it bluntly, *turned on,* on a whole mess of levels. This study goes a long way toward explaining why we have written records throughout history of many mystico-erotic gasps.

Here's the fascinating thing: All those intense mystico-erotic experiences reported by the Carmelite nuns and by the lovers in Wade's study are actually a natural part of our organic wiring. In other words, sexualized divinity ain't something otherworldly, or rare, or impossible for you to access, or only for people with blue eyes and type AB blood who were born at midnight on a Tuesday during a leap year when the constellation Orion was visible in the northern hemisphere. Andrew Newberg, scientist at the University of Pennsylvania School of Medicine and author of *Why God Won't Go*

 146

⇒ Reach Out and Touch Faith ⇐

Who first brought the notion of a mystico-erotic connection to God into the previously ascetic, de-sexed Church? Why, women, of course. Many scholars believe two powerful nuns in particular, Julian of Norwich (1342–1416) and Teresa of Avila (1515–1582), helped usher in a whole new perspective on the inherent sexuality of the divine connection; both women claimed to have personally experienced the divine sensually and sexually, via their physical bodies, experiences that led many within the Church to assume they were mistaking God for the devil (and oh, how very wrong they were).

In short, these nuns believed God could be and quite often was experienced as an erotic energy. To them, the body was not a hindrance to divine connection but actually a sacred place where we can become more familiar, more intimate with the divine. Julian and Teresa wrote about the body and our sexuality as good, natural, and divine (and God bless 'em for it), notions that, of course, didn't sit very well with the early church fathers, as we shall soon see.

Away: Brain Science and the Biology of Belief, has found that spiritual experiences are interwoven with human biology. (The scientific study of the effects of spiritual experiences on the human body is called *neurotheology.*) Newberg theorizes that the capacity for mystical experience is actually a by-product of sexual development. Which leads *The Red Book* to hypothesize that the more sexually aware you are, the higher your potential for divine connection. Other researchers theorize that our capacity for mystical experience may have evolved right alongside the brain networks involved in sexual pleasure. While mystical prayer and sexual bliss have their differences, they actually share neural pathways in the body.

So there you go. There is now plenty of fascinating scientific evidence that our physical biology supports and even encourages our divinity and also that sexual feelings might be more solidly linked to the divine than we realized. To which all the ancient, sexually vivid gods and goddesses reply, "Well, *duh.*"

Frisky Deities

Bob Francoeur, a professor in human sexuality at Fairleigh Dickinson University and editor of *The International Encyclopedia of Sexuality,* says that sexuality and spirituality have *always* been linked, from the beginning of the human race. In other words, the divine has been getting it on since time immemorial. For instance, the Babylonian goddess Ishtar seduced a mortal man, Gilgamesh. In Canaan, the chief god El had sex with the goddess Asherah. In Egyptian religions, the god Osiris had sex with his sister, the great goddess Isis. The Hindu god Krishna had sex with countless women, often at the same time, as he just multiplied himself (Hey, he's a god. Why have one orgasm, when you can have thousands, simultaneously?), but more commonly with his true love, the mortal woman Radha. Annual pre-Christian rituals in Europe often involved sexual rites among the peasants that celebrated the sacred marriage between god and

goddess and that were believed to promote the fertility of the land. In ancient Greece, Zeus was married to the goddess Hera, but he also seduced untold numbers of mortal women, and when he wasn't chasing skirts, was known to be a frequent masturbator. (In fact, Greek myth is packed with tawdry god-human sexual encounters, from Aphrodite to *The Odyssey,* including much homoerotic sex.) Let's stop here, because the list of sexually explicit divine exploits throughout history is indeed endless.

Only during the last 2,000 years of Western civilization have sexuality and spirituality been forcibly separated and made to appear to be enemies. Francoeur says the split between sexuality and spirituality emerged from the Greek philosophy of dualism (the mind-body split), and other scholars believe that the separation was solidified with the rise of monotheistic, male-dominated traditions (Judaism, Christianity, Islam). Even though pre-Christian Hebrews were not anti-sexuality or anti-body (they saw both as gifts from God), God was de-sexed within the Jewish Torah (in which Creation just sort of happened when God said the word; there was no juicy hanky-panky of fertilization, no great cosmic orgasm that seeded this universe, as was the case in numerous pagan traditions), and Jewish and Christian leaders taught, of course, that sex should be reserved for marriage, and, even then, only for procreation. And although marriage is one of the seven sacraments of Catholicism, it was ranked a distant third, after virginity and, uh, widowhood in terms of spiritual priorities expounded by many of the early church fathers. Sad to say, in far too many religions, the repression of sexuality is usually linked directly with the repression of women. Why? Read on.

Sex Is Sin, Woman Is Sex

According to scholar Kee Boem Bo in his article "Sexuality as a Locus of Spirituality," early Christianity developed intense eroto-phobia (fear of the erotic) and quickly associated sexuality with sin. A big chunk of this tragically erroneous belief came from none other than St. Augustine (384–386), one of the most influential of the early church fathers, who felt that sexual desire was contrary to the control of the mind or will and a direct result of original sin. (You remember that one, right? When Eve and Adam fell from God's grace by chomping on that apple that fateful, snaky day, way back when?) Even though eating forbidden fruit was not specifically sex-ual, Augustine theologized that its effects caused Adam and Eve to lose control of their bodies and their willpower, which is what *led* to wanton sex. And now, of course, all of humanity participates in this horribly shameful sin. Augustine believed that if we could hold off our prurient urges, think about baseball and our grandmothers when they arose, and commit to virginity, then we would be greatly rewarded in heaven (or laughed at by promiscuous angels: "What the hell were you guys *thinking?* Saving yourself? For what? Purity is a state of *mind,* not a state of the body. Now come over here and let me show you how to truly feel God"). Ahem. So anyway, for a variety of painful and unfortunate reasons, virginity and celibacy soon became the highest standards for spiritual purity in the Church.

This was also right around the time (400 C.E. or so) when the Catholic Church created the theological myth of the *Virgin* Mary. In sum, when women desired a close relationship with God, they were

PURITY IS A STATE OF MIND

told to look toward the Virgin Mary as their role model. Now, there's a good one to look up to: the mother of God, someone who was supposedly the most perfect, untainted woman to have ever existed, who ostensibly never craved a kiss or had naughty thoughts. Right. We can all totally relate. And to demonize women's sexuality even more, in 591, Pope Gregory declared Mary Magdalene a prostitute (which, by the way, was just flat-out wrong; the early church fathers conflated Mary Magdalene with *three* other women, one of them who was *supposedly* a prostitute. But this dangerous, erroneous despoliation of Mary Magdalene wasn't revoked by the Church for another 1,500 years, until 1969). The bottom line: If you were a woman during those 1,500 years, you were one of two things: a virgin or a whore. Sounds a little like high school, no? Astounding how long these bogus notions linger in the culture.

Scholar Richard Hooker tells us that St. Jerome (340–420), another dominant early church father, whose texts were hugely influential in defining gender roles in the Church, believed that women were nothing but bad news. Because they were not ruled by reason, female passions were uncontrollable; hence, women degraded men by luring them toward sin. Jerome used biblical stories (which were themselves interpretations, rewritten by men) to prove his point. For example, Samson and David (two of God's favorites) fell from favor in the Lord's eyes because they were seduced by two pagan women, Delilah and Bathsheba. But what Jerome failed to recognize was that these women came from cultures that encouraged sexual acts as a form of *celebration* of the gods (though not, of course, the Christian monotheistic god). For many in these cultures, consenting sex was just another way of shouting "Hallelujah!"

151

Another giant in the early Church whose most significant legacy to early religion was his fierce hatred of women? St. Ambrose (340–397). He was the one who decreed that women couldn't hold any sort of high church office (that is, become priests)—despite other Christian movements, like Gnosticism, that did have female leaders—because of our rampant, uncontrollable sexuality. Women's lustful nature was, of course, a fundamental flaw that, again, led men to temptation. (Notice how many early Christian teachings seldom make men responsible for any sexual slips? Apparently, *we* are the ones with all the control issues and unquenchable lust.) Ambrose is on my top ten list of dead people to spank because, according to scholars like Richard Hooker, he's responsible for introducing a radical new element to early Christian misogyny. He equated female sexuality with female inferiority, and this idea has influenced the Church for hundreds of years, even filtering down to the present day. (Female priests have recently been allowed in a few Christian denominations but still not in Catholicism.) The misogyny spawned by the early Church has died down a great deal, but it still exists, subtly yet powerfully. Do I sound a little bitter? Nah. After all, those prudish men are being reformed. I have it in good confidence that they've been recently introduced to apple-flavored Eros sexual lubricant by none other than Kali herself.

Dutiful Orgasms

Let's slip on over to the third Big Daddy monotheistic religion: Islam. Despite a pervasive general Islamic view that sex is shameful

⬳ Did Jesus Get His Groove On? ⬳

Early Christians weren't *all* so prudish. Remember the Gnostics? They often used sexual symbolism when describing the divine and are partially responsible for the current hot debate about whether Jesus and Mary Magdalene were ever sitting in a tree, K-I-S-S-I-N-G. In fact, the Gnostic Gospel of Phillip quite blatantly says, ". . . The companion of the Savior is Mary Magdalene. But Christ loved her more than all the disciples, and used to kiss her often on the mouth." The disciples asked Jesus, "Why do you love her more than all of us?" I'll venture an answer: Perhaps because she was an intelligent, spiritually awake woman who really "got" JC. (By the way, the gospels often imply that Jesus wasn't always so pleased with the learning abilities of his male disciples.)

There is still much debate about the possible love affair between Jesus and Mary Magdalene (scholars *always* need more tangible proof), but everyone does agree that Mary was Jesus' dear friend. Many Gnostics believed she was also his most advanced spiritual disciple, to whom Jesus passed his most secret, esoteric, and mystical teachings. According to the Gnostics, Jesus wanted Mary to spread these secrets and teach others. Of course, some of Jesus' male disciples became jealous, and *something* made Mary flee. Sadly, most of those teachings fled with her. Interesting side note: In traditional Christian paintings, the Magdalene is typically portrayed wearing *red* robes or with fiery *red* hair. Fancy that.

153

and dirty (an attitude often attributed to the early influence of Christianity), there are a few verses in the Koran, the holy book of Islam, that actually *encourage* married couples to enjoy sexual relations. Crazy. After all, the founder of Islam, the prophet Muhammad, was said to enjoy much physical satisfaction and affection with his wives. (Well, it's about time we heard about a major spiritual leader's sex life that's not solely based on procreation, right?) Different *hadith*—written narrations of the sayings and practices of the Prophet—state that it's actually a woman's *right* to have an orgasm and that sexual dissatisfaction is legitimate grounds for divorcing a husband. *Now* we're talking. But of course, in many Islamic cultures, this information has been buried pretty deeply, and, more often than not, sexuality is seen as something that needs to be controlled or hidden or mastered, most often by men. Alas.

The Other Side of the Cosmic Bed

The West is not the only part of this beautiful globe with far too many sexual-spiritual hang-ups. Oh no, this sticky issue has been sweated in *all* the world's religions. Many Hindu and Buddhist traditions believe the body and physical desire (and the women who, of course, represent these) are roadblocks to enlightenment and therefore need to be transcended. There are passages in some early Buddhist sutras and Hindu texts in which women are described as overly passionate, hateful, or even stupid and their bodies are seen as impure and shameful, and in some texts, Buddha warns his followers not to even *look* at women. But by and large, the East has

154

had *much* more libidinous fun than the West, not to mention far fewer restrictions when it comes to sexuality.

Perhaps the most famous example of the East's openness to all things sexual is the Kama Sutra. Maybe you've heard of it? This intensely detailed, carefully diagrammed erotic love guide originated in India around the third century B.C.E., well over 2,000 years ago. Although Western versions of the Kama Sutra have been much diluted (pop culture has reduced this complex, exquisite sutra to a simplistic book of sexual positions), the original is far more elaborate than you might imagine. The original Kama Sutra not only includes tantalizing descriptions of the sixty-four sexual positions but features advice on how to be a good citizen and how to handle yourself in a relationship, along with detailed grooming hints designed to make you an attractive, intelligent, and sensual woman, covering such topics as beading necklaces, tattooing, archery, storing water, replacing stained glass, studying different languages and vocabulary, writing poetry, coloring your teeth, dancing, participating in "youthful" sports, magic and sorcery, cock fighting, chemistry, architecture, reciting mathematical equations, and teaching a parrot to talk. Now *that's* a sex guide.

But while the Kama Sutra may be one of the most well known texts, the world's earliest known sex manuals were from China. These poignant works, many based in Taoism, not only prescribe having sex as much as possible but also advocate prolonging the sex act as *long* as possible, all as a means to achieving immortality. These early masters, too, believed that the man must, without fail, rouse the woman to orgasm because when both man and woman were satisfied, the dual energies of yin-yang are brought into harmony.

(Yin and yang are the two overarching principles of the universe, according to Taoism, China's ancient spiritual philosophy. Yin is the feminine, yang is the masculine, and each contains a seed of the other.) In fact, sexual intercourse was believed to be one of the main roads to heaven.

By the way, Taoism isn't the only spiritual tradition that emphasizes the importance of working with and uniting the masculine and the feminine energies. Tantric sects of Buddhism and Hinduism, as well as parts of Gnosticism and Jewish Kabbalah, encourage this sacred union as well. Many of the mystical and indigenous traditions of the world have always recognized that the divine universe has an erotic charge, one that can be felt and encouraged in the body during sex but also during meditation or by just being conscious and receptive to the natural world.

Tantra Unites

According to the philosophy of Tantra, the universe is a manifestation of pure consciousness. There is *nothing* that isn't divine. Everything is interrelated, interconnected, and everything affects everything else. Tantra tells us that this pure, universal consciousness has two interdependent poles: the *Shiva* (masculine) energy, which is "unmanifest" and static and has the power to be, but not to become, and the *Shakti* (feminine) energy, which is dynamic, energetic, and creative. She becomes. She is also seen as the *Maha Devi* (Great Mother) of the universe. According to Tantra, the human being is a universe in miniature; all that is found out there in the cosmos can be found right here inside us, so the same principles that apply to the external universe apply to the internal one.

Is It Porn or a Road Map to Enlightenment?

In India, the enormous, ornate Chandela religious temples of Khajuraho (in central India) contain stunningly explicit sex scenes carved into the very temple walls themselves. Couples and groups copulate in all manner of orgiastic revelry. There's even a horse involved in one scene! Is this the earliest form of pornography? Not quite. Many believe that these are ancient illustrations of how to attain enlightenment. Other scholars think the temples are more likely connected to the practice of sacred prostitution, which was a lucrative business for many temples at that time. (Select men and women who were considered to be married to the temple's deity would sometimes offer sex to commoners and kings alike, in order to give laypeople a special spiritual connection to the divine.)

When I was studying in Tibet, I went with a group of students to visit a sacred monastery that was built on an island in the middle of a lake. When we arrived at the monastery entrance, our jaws dropped, because flanking one side of the great door was a very detailed, enormous (at least four feet high) plaster representation of a vagina. Sure enough, the other side boasted an equally enormous, erect penis. Our professor explained to us (quickly and quietly, before the beaming monks could register our shock) that these sacred icons represented the fundamental creative and spiritual powers of the universe and were regarded as intensely powerful and necessary to incorporate into one's individual spiritual path. (I have some really great photos from that particular day.)

Or as the *Vishvasara Tantra* states, "What is Here, is Elsewhere. What is not Here, is Nowhere." The goal in Tantra is to unite Shiva and Shakti, the masculine with the feminine, and transcend *all* dualisms to experience enlightened bliss. Simple enough, right? Ever see that very popular iconic image or statue of a seated male deity with a female deity sitting in his lap, legs wide apart, embracing him? This is the common representation of this great male-female union, called, appropriately, *Shiva-shakti* or, in Tibetan Buddhism, *Yab Yum.* And oh yes, they're having sex.

In Tantra, consciousness is not just in the mind; it permeates the physical body too, making the body not just a fleshy thing that our spirits have to drag around this planet or an obstacle to the divine but a living, moving road map to and temple of divinity. (Man alive, is *that* a little different than what I was taught about my body by Sister Mary Agnes way back in Sunday school.) But FYI, true Tantric sexual rituals require an *immense* amount of spiritual training and are extremely technical and quite different than the slightly shallow versions you might find in *Cosmo* ("10 Tantric Sex Secrets to Make Him Moan"). According to Andre Van Lysebeth, author of *Tantra: The Cult of the Feminine,* to a tantrist, pleasure and enjoyment are not self-serving or meant just to satisfy the ego, because a tantrist knows that Shakti (the active female energy) experiences pleasure through the tantrist and is already embodied within the tantrist. In other words, when you experience pleasure, the divine experiences pleasure; you work as a blissful, co-dependent team.

ROAD MAP TO DIVINITY

⇒ Before You Go Traditionally Tantric ⇒

Quick note: It must be said, the world's great religious traditions are not, at their core, necessarily misogynistic or specifically anti-sexual. While there were certainly a number of strict, old-school traditionalists who coded these harsh beliefs into their religion, many modern believers are seeking to dispel their ugly influence, so the beautiful, wise sexual hearts of the religions can beat naturally again.

What's more, despite how wonderful many of those Tantric and Taoist beliefs sound, they have not always translated so wonderfully into lived experience, often due to the patriarchal culture surrounding them. Despite the reverence for the *divine* feminine energy and holistic sexual symbolism, ordinary women and real sexuality are often not held in as high esteem. But with a little work, honest intent, and love, we can take inspiration from these ancient beliefs and learn how to translate them into our own lives.

Turn Your Self On

All right, enough history, enough research. Whew. Hopefully, you've gained a bit of an idea as to why sexuality has been considered such a taboo, why so many traditions have tried to ignore or repress it, and why some of us, despite our liberal, open-minded ways and even our nonparticipation in traditional religions (we're still exposed to

159

them culturally just by being Americans), might still feel a little strange about associating sexuality with our spirituality. I hope that all that background also revealed how uniting those two wonderful parts of our selves (male and female, yin and yang, body and spirit, universe and Universe, human self and God self) is one of the most natural and enlightening things to do in the world.

But in order to realize how enlightening sex and sexuality can be, not only do we have to shake ourselves free from all that religion-based misogyny, but we also have to release ourselves from other modern sources of sexual misinformation. Yes, women have come a long way, and yes, we live in a culture that has a more lenient attitude toward female sexuality, but that doesn't mean that most of us are clear from sexual static cling. It almost goes without saying that as young women in America, our sexuality is deeply affected by the media, social mores, stereotypes, "flawless" Photoshopped fashion models, submissive girlfriend roles, and other unhealthy BS. Many of us have deep wounds concerning our sexuality, either due to a repressive upbringing or a history of various kinds of sexual abuse. Many of us also have some deep insecurities and inhibitions, intensified by hypersexualized messages from our culture that equate worth with sexiness. What's more, many of us, for whatever reason, cannot have a genuine orgasm, or we take on every lover we can in an attempt to heal some deep loneliness, or we're just completely unconscious about our sexuality for a variety of complex and sometimes deeply emotional reasons. I know. We've been through a lot. All this is why becoming more attuned and aware of your unique sexuality, being willing to look under your covers and shine a little divine light on whatever you find, can be an incredibly important and healing spiritual practice.

A Whole Bunch of Sex Questions

This much we know: Sexuality is an organic, natural part of being human, of being alive. And when we aren't conscious about it, or when we deny it, or when we are ashamed of it or unhealthy with it or just take it for granted and don't really pay much attention to it, we miss out on an *incredibly* vital piece of life, an intimate experience and expression of who we are and, thus, a powerful way to experience divinity.

Think you're ready to get a bit more up close and personal with your unique sexuality? I hope you are. Could you use some help? I have a suggestion: Try discussing some of the following questions with friends, your lover, or a therapist, or even writing out your answers in your red book. You'll be amazed at how healthy and helpful it can be just to get your sexual feelings out there, even if you already feel more or less OK with your sexuality.

- How did your parents, siblings, and friends respond to your first sexual questions, attitudes, and experiences when you were a child? (Remember "I'll show you mine if you show me yours" and "Doctor"?)
- What did you know about your parents' sexual relationship, if anything?
- Have you ever seriously combined spirituality and sex—say, in the same sentence or the same bed?

- What was your first sexual experience like? Was it satisfying? Did it make you feel good about yourself? Why or why not? What have you learned about yourself and your sexual body since then?
- Do you have a vibrator? Do you use it? If not, why?
- Have you ever felt shame about your body or about your sexuality? Why, or with whom?
- What's your impression of portrayals of sex and women's sexuality in the media (film, magazines, TV, Internet)? Do they empower you? Make you feel insecure? A little of both? If you were in charge, how would you do it differently?
- Do you use your sexuality for control or manipulation or to gain power or respect or acceptance, or do you use it to spread love? Are you even *aware* of how you use it?
- Have you ever felt any sort of spiritual, energetic opening during sex? What was it like?
- How have you worked on healing any negative sexual experiences? Do you need to work on them more? How will you go about making sure you do this?
- Are you able to communicate your sexual needs and cravings easily and honestly with your partner? If not, why? What would happen if you did? Right now?

Whew. All right, that was a lot. But so is sexuality. As a friend of mine says, when it comes to sex, if you can't talk about it, maybe you shouldn't be doing it. Spend some quality time with your self and keep creating more questions. Unpeel more layers.

Temple Yourself to Find Your Self

OK, one last question: What do you think you could do, right now, to start making your sexuality more at home within your body, your relationships, your spirituality? How about a massage (giving or receiving) or other intense body work? It's a start. Or exploring belly dance, hula hoop, or strip tease? Or maybe getting into kundalini yoga, wherein you focus on slowly raising your kundalini—a reserve of potent female Shakti energy located at the base of your spine—to the top of your head, to unite with the male Shiva energy, in order to unite the body, mind, and spirit? Hell, do *any* form of physical exercise to get the blood flowing.

What else can you do? Practice speaking positively to your body, no matter how bloated you feel. Ask your favorite goddess or the universe for help, to highlight areas of your sexuality that need some attention. Perform a ritual to help you let go of a painful sexual experience. Punctuate your meditations with an orgasm (or vice versa), or meditate on orgasms, or turn your orgasms into a meditation. (Does that seem slightly transgressive? Good!) If you're normally shy or inhibited about your body, take a deep breath and maybe have a glass of red wine, then try communicating your sexual needs and fantasies—directly, explicitly—to your lover, or even just say the words, aloud, to yourself. Skinny dip. Sleep naked. Play in the mud. Invest in a high-quality sex toy or three, and become your own best lover. Educate yourself, read some female-centric empowering sex books, go to some lectures or workshops, visit a sex therapist or a woman-friendly sex store or Web site (see the resource section). Write a sizzling love poem to your body. Create a list of the top ten best places to touch yourself and stick it on your refrigerator door. Revise the list every week. What if you treated yourself like a goddess for a day? What would you do? How would you feed yourself, take care of yourself, revere yourself? What sort of prayers would you create? What sort of rituals? What would your name be? What would you wear? Who would you allow to worship you? How would you expect to be treated?

Is that too much? Feeling a little overwhelmed with all the possibilities? I know what you mean. But this is the thing about divine energy: It's *supposed* to be everywhere. See, sexuality is less about the actual *act* of having pretty good sex for seventeen minutes twice a week and much more about surrounding yourself with an ever-simmering sensual *energy,* pulsing just underneath your daily life and infusing almost everything you do. It's like you're always just a little bit horny, just a little turned on, but the object of your gentle lust isn't just your lover, it's divine life itself.

And let's be clear: *The Red Book* is not encouraging you to become some stereotypical *Cosmo* sex goddess, but it is encouraging you to be a goddess of your unique sexuality. Just like *The Red Book* is not interested in telling you *how* to be spiritual, I'm not interested in telling you exactly *how* to be sexual, either. I merely offer a few suggestions to help you become more familiar with your sexual-spiritual self, in the hope that they might inspire you to create your own unique approaches ("Treat myself like a goddess, my ass, that's for airy-fairy girls; I want to treat myself like an active volcano!"). *The Red Book* is not trying to set a particular standard of sexuality against which your spirituality should be measured. It is encouraging you to witness whether and how this divine intervention changes your experiences or shifts your perspectives. Above all, it's important to become more conscious and honor our sexual truths, no matter what they might look like to others or to the culture around us.

Jade Stalks and Lotus Flowers

These days you can find numerous people who are reconnecting sex and spirit, often through incredibly loose interpretations of Tantra. I'm talking about twinkling candles and heady flowers and staring meaningfully into your lover's eyes as you try to sync up your breathing and feel each other's heartbeats, all while referring to the vagina as *yoni* or *lotus flower* and the penis as *lingam* or *jade stalk*

☞ Take a Break Already ☜

Sometimes we just need a major sexual time-out, to be in the world in a way that's not always so sexually charged. Yes, I'm talking about voluntary celibacy, a practice that, despite its monkish connotations, can actually, with the right intention and self-guided time limit, provide an incredibly powerful opportunity for you to get to know a whole other divine side of your self.

Celibacy certainly has its time and place. Maybe you are just coming out of a painful breakup, are healing from an illness or trauma, or have been misusing sex in a way that you know could use a rest. Or maybe you just aren't feelin' it during a particular time in your life. Respect yourself; trust your body. All too often, we're made to feel like we *have* to be sexual just because we're young women, and that can be just as repressive as anything.

Sometimes we just need a break from it all in order to focus on rounding out our lives, on being a woman who is free from the sexual status quo, a woman who is respecting her own boundaries and learning how to nourish her divine self through other means. And then, when the time is right, we step back into the sexual whirlpool, but with a clearer, healthier, more self-aware attitude.

(Hindu Tantric and Taoist terms). And then, finally, you get to actually have sex, which could quite possibly last a really long time, because the focus is on prolonged orgasms and awakening the woman's G-spot. (Sting wasn't exaggerating much when he boasted that he and his wife Trudi had Tantric sex for seven hours straight— except that it wasn't exactly sex as you might regularly imagine it. It was more like a sustained sexual energy.)

While these sorts of practices can be enriching, I want to go on record as saying that you certainly don't have to light candles or use exotic names for your genitalia or find your G-spot in order to connect with the divine. What *is* important is trying to be as *conscious* during sex as you would during any other part of your spiritual practice. Conscious sex can heal, help us release stuck emotions and energy patterns, and bring us closer to our lovers. It can make us feel, well, more *alive*. In present time. All senses turned on high. And that's a place I just know the divine likes to touch.

So then, how to start cultivating an empowering sexual consciousness? Start by setting your intention. That's right, you can *intend* to be conscious, divinely aware, healthy and fearless in your skin as you have sex. In the bedroom, you can try holding the present-moment calm and connective awareness that you may sense during meditation. Pay attention and respond to signs your partner is giving or that your own body is exhibiting. Treat your body as divine. Treat the body of your lover as divine. To put it simply, don't just go through your regular motions in bed; *be aware* of the divine energy swirling around you as you have sex. That awareness can make all the difference.

You can calmly dedicate any and every beautiful sexual escapade to the universe ("Let this act generate love, peace, and passionate aliveness for the whole planet"), sans any woo-woo chanting and fluff. Try this: Before having sex, take a few deep breaths and really ground yourself, connect yourself to the room and the bed and the moment, feel the fabric and soak up the colors and smell the sheets and really *focus*, and set your intent for a healthy, blissful connective experience.

And hey, some of the best creative prayers can emerge even *while* you're having sex. Whilst in the throes next time (alone or with a lover), just close your eyes for a moment and focus on that white-hot ball of divine energy that the sex is stirring up inside you, and allow all that divine love you hold to bubble up and to pour out and flood all over you, your partner, your apartment, your city block, the country, the world (even, or maybe especially, any of those early repressive religious figures from any and all religions). I mean this literally. Really imagine this loving energy, like some sort of warm light or heated breath or epiphanic sound spreading out, all over. Experience the divine in a literal, physical sense, right there in your hands, in your very fingertips, all the way down to your pinky toes. After all, you are divinity fleshed, and the goal is to fuse body and spirit into one, like a gorgeous perfume, a fine whiskey, the perfect blend of you.

Body Wise

Igniting your divine spark is about *embodiment*—horizontal transcendence with a twist. It is about grounding all the spiritual theory and awareness straight into your flesh. It's also, even more important, about drawing your innate divine power straight *out* of your wiggly and tingly cells and creatively releasing it out into the world. It's about learning how to appreciate the body as a very real, living, breathing, wise presence of divinity. It's about allowing all the mysterious, corporeal energies you may have been taught were inappropriate or shameful out into the light. Remember, sexuality is not just the act of sex; it's a passionate attitude, an exchange of loving energy, a way of engaging the world on a fully appreciative, deeply sensual level. It's just one more part of you that opens up to the divine and says ahhh.

CHAPTER 12

Sitting Down and Shutting Up

The Best Spiritual Tool You Will Ever Learn, Ever (Except for the One in Chapter Thirteen)

Remember how annoyed you get when you're on the phone with your significant other, and you can tell that he or she's busy doing something else—surfing the Web, watching TV, cooking or cleaning? Or how 'bout when you're out eating dinner with your best friend and telling her the most amazing thing that has happened to you that day, but she keeps glancing over your shoulder, checking out the drama of the couple behind you? Yep, no real connection. The conversation just isn't getting the energy it deserves, and what's more, you can feel it. Well, this is probably close to what our spirit feels like 99 percent of the time—wishing that we would tune in enough to receive our own wisdom.

Like any relationship, the one between you and your divine spark needs a lot of good ol' quality time. You need to cultivate it. As spiritual teacher Marianne Williamson says, it's much like the people close to you: If you really want to be a great friend, you sit with them and focus your attention and really *listen*. And since your relationship with the divine is essentially your relationship with your deeper self, you do indeed need to sit with yourself and really listen, nurturing the relationship as often as you can. And one of the best ways to do it? You guessed it: meditation.

It's true, and it's very simple. Nothing helps you know your divine spark better than sitting still and quieting your mind. Not talking with your friends or reading books or listening to holy people or having amazing sex or pondering the meaning of life while soaking in your bathtub. This is why meditation is part of every spiritual tradition on this planet, and why it lies at the heart of *The Red Book*.

Become More Buddha-full

At its core, the practice of meditation helps focus the mind and keep you in the present moment by quieting all the external stimuli and directing your attention inward, often through concentrating on a specific image, sound, word, or movement or simply on your own breath. Where you take it from this point depends on which specific practice you're drawn to. Meditation in its many variations can help you, the practitioner, dissolve your ego, commune with some form of the divine, focus the process of self-realization (onion peeling), understand your inner "Buddha nature" (your true nature, the eternal source that dwells inside you that allows awakening and enlightenment), hang tight with your divine spark, or, better yet, all of the above.

As if those weren't good enough reasons to dive into the wonderfully enlightening habit of regular meditation, modern-day Janes (that would be us) have some new incentives to go lotus. Meditation's powerful healing effects have now been scientifically and medically proven. No matter whether you're an absolute beginner or an eighty-year-old monk, meditation's benefits are irrefutable. A few of the problems and issues regular meditation can reduce include anxiety, physical pain, depression, stress, insomnia, PMS and menstrual cramps, acne, and migraines. Meditation can improve the quality of your sleep, improve physical stamina, and help hone the cognitive function of your brain, all while improving the body's ability to heal and slow down the effects of aging. Meditation can also help build self-confidence, enhance the immune system, boost your level of seratonin (the chemical in the brain that makes you feel elated and ecstatic), help resolve phobias, and calm fears and neurosis. Now, don't get too excited. Despite all the amazing claims, meditation isn't the ultimate magic bullet, but it's definitely one of the most powerful tools in your spiritual belt.

Meditation provides the space and time for you to assimilate, to metabolize all the spiritual ideas and concepts you've been learning, so that you can start translating them into lived experience. More important, meditation helps you recognize the endless well of spiritual wisdom and love right inside yourself. Once the Buddha was asked, "Is there God?" The Buddha answered, "I will not tell you. But, if you wish, I can show you how to find out for yourself." Then he taught the person meditation. Once you experience your essential divine nature, you have no more false sense of separation. You know you're hooked up. You know the divine can never be truly absent, because it's essentially who you really are. This awareness is, perhaps, meditation's greatest benefit of all.

My First (But Not My Last) Zen Spanking

When I was nineteen years old, I went on my first weeklong Zen meditation retreat, and it was pretty hard-core. We had to get up every day at 4:30 A.M. and sit cross-legged in lotus position for two hours of silent meditation. We then ate breakfast in silence, cleaned the joint, had some instruction, then ate lunch in silence. After lunch

GO LOTUS

came more meditation, followed by a silent dinner and yet one more session of meditation before bed. Good times.

On the last day of the retreat, we were allowed a private meeting with the Zen master, during which we were allowed one question. I can't remember all of what I asked—I think sheer embarrassment, thankfully, has blocked my memory—but it was something along these lines: "So I've been studying all these religions and philosophies and New Age ideas, and I'm still just so confused; I mean, is the divine Jesus or Buddha or energy, or is it a great Void of Nothingness; and how do I know which belief system is *my* belief system, because I really don't want to get this wrong; and I can feel the divine when I eat pizza if I am open to it, so why do I have to meditate; and what is enlightenment, and should I even be trying for it, because it sounds blissful and all but also really damn boring, and I like dancing and sex and clothes a lot; in fact, I like being human a lot, but is that just my ego speaking or might I be hitting on something true; and why do I have to stay in the present moment to know my essential divine nature; and how come you guys get up so early in the morning, and what's with the celibacy, and why do bees buzz, and when's dinner . . . ?" Sounds a little crazy, right? The scary thing is, I think it was actually worse than that.

The Zen master just sat still for a while, as I prepared myself for what had to be an epic answer. He slowly raised his head, looked me squarely in the eyes, and calmly said, "You need to sit and shut up." Then he rang his little bell, signifying that our time had ended. I was floored. Dumbfounded. Not to mention hugely embarrassed. I was also a little outraged and felt more than a little gypped. That was it? Sit and shut up? You call that an answer? How rude is that?

INHALE

Who needs Zen? I can hear that sort of stuff from my mother! Needless to say, I was a little confused.

Now, of course, years later, I get it. He couldn't answer any of those questions for me. Only I could. What's more, perhaps those types of questions didn't really *need* to be answered. They weren't actually the point at all. And the best way for me to realize all of this was to literally sit, which means "meditate" to those Zen monastics, and shut my busy, frothing mind up. That's it. Now that master, *he* was a good teacher.

Monkey Mind

Eastern spiritualities are home to some of the most well-developed practices of meditation. According to Buddhism and Hinduism in particular, meditation is the process of training, developing, and purifying the chaotic mind—which is often described as a wild monkey—so we learn how to master it and not let it master us. These forms of meditation train you to distinguish between what is merely your analytical mind and your ego personality, and your true essence.

Here's a quick exercise in Eastern-style meditation: Take a few deep breaths and relax your body, then let your breath return to normal and start paying close attention to it. Start a slow numeric count for each inhale, and then exhale, with a small pause at the top and the bottom of the breath, but try to do so without too much thinking (except for the count). Every time you have a thought, any thought (I have to call Mom; my back is sore; this book is crazy; hey, look, here's me trying not to have a thought), empty the breath and start the count over. Do this as many times as it takes until you can observe at least one entire breath cycle (one full inhalation and exhalation) without any thought whatsoever, just the calm observation of the rise and fall of the breath in the lungs. Once you make it through one breath, try it for two, then maybe three. (If you can do ten really slow breath cycles without a single thought flittering in, you're nearly a master and should put this book down right now and start teaching the rest of us.)

I was taught this beginner's meditation at the Zen monastery, and it's more difficult than it appears. In fact, most of us can only focus for a couple breaths at a time before the mind races back in. The monkey mind is powerful indeed. But the point of this kind of meditation is not to try and up your breath count every time, trying to beat your previous time, like it's the high score in a video game. The point is to help you quiet your internal dialogue or at least recognize it for the crazy monkey that it is. Often when we simply acknowledge our extreme head trips for what they are and quietly watch them do their little break-dance, without judgment or forced control, the mind soon calms down on its own, almost automatically.

The point of all this internal shushing is that many spiritual traditions believe that the divine, or our essential Buddha nature, is most profoundly and directly experienced in the space *between* our thoughts—that is, it's in the being, not the doing; in the receiving, not the grabbing. In complete stillness. In total silence. One of the great ironies of modern culture is how we think we're being so intelligent by thinking all the time, by multitasking and planning and juggling a hundred phone calls and ideas and evening plans.

EXHALE

177

⇒ Thanks for Sharing, Buh-Bye ⇒

We all have a million thoughts running through our mind, and merely deciding we want them to stop is not going to make it so. Just know that at the beginning of just about any meditation practice, you will have plenty of thoughts pinballing around in your head, no matter how soft your focus. This is fine and normal. One thing to do is simply acknowledge them, say hello, and then let them pass by like a cloud in the sky. Or as many spiritual teachers suggest, when a thought rushes in, urgent to be heard, simply say, "Thanks for sharing" and then let it go.

But the spiritual masters say we only become *truly* wise when we have the power to *separate* from our thoughts. This is because the divine, or Ultimate Reality, or who you really are, cannot be grasped with your rational monkey mind. So if the divine is not best experienced through your thoughts, yet you're thinking nonstop, just how do you suppose you two are going to become one? Ponder that one for a while. Or better yet, don't.

Opening Your Present

When we learn to soothe the rambunctious monkey and experience conscious stillness through meditation, we're able to live more in the moment, with full awareness. And if all the great spiritual masters agree on one thing, it's that the here and now is the *only* place where divinity or the eternal source truly resides. But the snag is, most of us are quite far from that moment, even right now, as you read these words.

Yep, all too often we're zipping off to the future or dwelling on the past. We're constantly making plans, revising our to-do lists, reliving past episodes, allowing our thoughts to wander almost anywhere but to the immediate moment at hand. When we're riding the subway, we're thinking about last night's late-night phone call from you know who. While we're at a meeting, we're busy thinking about what we're gonna make for dinner or what we're gonna say after so-and-so stops gabbing. When we're visiting our family, instead of being present to what is really going on—a relatively peaceful and calm get-together—we keep pondering past fights, reliving old woundings, feeling all those old hoary power dynamics re-emerge, and so we keep ourselves as guarded and snarky as when we were kids. And even when we meditate, we start imagining just how great our future star-spangled enlightenment could be, instead of just being OK with where we are right now, sitting calmly, breathing deeply, feeling alive and well.

The problem with constant mental fidgeting, with constantly being out of our own bodies is how we tend to let the chains of the past and the pressures of the future keep us from radiating right now. If we're not fully present, then we miss life's ordinary magic, its profound moments, subtle divine signs, and revelatory intuitive nudges. We stop being spontaneous and original. We become mere reflections of our same old patterns, or we act based on assumptions or expectations or on things that haven't even happened yet. As many of the wise ones say, nothing else exists but right now. All those memories and future worries are illusions; they are not real. But they can feel very real when we are not grounded in the now, when we don't keep ourselves awake and ready.

When we forget to be present in the moment, we miss the sacred experience of a human *being*. We forget that God is deeply present in the moments of life, embedded within the details—even your gabby coworker's overdone presentation or your dad's constant pressuring about 401k's or your cat's insistence on sitting atop your head while you read.

Meditation helps us practice staying present, so we can clearly see the truth of our situation and the divine potential in our everyday activities. We stop trying to transcend the material world or to fill it with explanations or complications, and learn to simply *be* with it, on its own terms. Likewise, when we're in the moment, we're able to be with the *body,* too, in its physical immediacy. By just doing the concrete things we do on a daily basis—like brushing our teeth, washing the dishes, walking to work—with awareness (Zen breathing practice can really help here), we're able to draw forth the richness from any and every experience. The ultimate ideal is for us to turn our lives into a moving meditation. We do what we always do, but while hosting an internal stillness, a continual present-time awareness of and direct connection with the Grand Hum of Us All.

What Shuts You Up?

These days, it seems that almost any body-centering, mind-calming practice or prayer gets lumped under the meditation umbrella, which I'm sure must make Buddha sigh and roll his third eye.

⪦ Ground Yourself ⪧

A helpful energetic technique that is taught by many esoteric schools, as well as by powerful alternative spiritual traditions like Wicca, is how to ground yourself. It's a way to reconnect to the planet, feel your feet planted solidly on terra firma, and root you in present time.

Here's what you do: Sit calmly in a strong-backed chair (or stand up) with your back straight and your feet on the ground. Close your eyes, slow your breath, and begin to imagine a super-strong connecting line—it can be a cord, a stone pillar, a tree trunk, a thick wire or chain, or whatever else suits your fancy—running down from your lower torso through the floor and through the soil and all the way down, down, down into the center of the earth, where the line connects to the earth's core like an anchor, immovable and so solid you can almost lean back in your chair (or on your heels, if you're standing) and feel it supporting you. You can practice this anytime and anywhere (well, maybe not on airplanes), though you may need to have your eyes open, of course.

So if you ever feel yourself to be out of balance during a confrontation or when you're speeding down a busy highway or talking with friends at a loud party or jogging in the woods, or if you keep misplacing things like your car keys, try this strengthening technique and see if you notice a difference in your sense of calmness, presence, and connection to the moment.

The great thing about all these practices is that at least one of them or maybe even a few should resonate with you.

Essentially, meditation practices can be split into two main types: passive and active. Passive meditation is sitting still and listening or just letting go. There's no particular focus but, rather, an emphasis on witnessing whatever is going on inside. It's like attending an inner home movie—simply watching yourself, seeing what's up for you today, but without becoming too attached to the outcome or the drama of the leading lady (that's you). Conversely, active meditation has similar goals of stillness and halting your mental chatter, but its methods of getting you there are, well, more active. You might recite a mantra (a sacred phrase or word or name of the divine, meant to be repeated over and over), or you might visualize a deity or mandala (a symbolic pictorial representation of the universe) or actively run energy up and down your spine or clear your chakras. You might practice rigorous yoga asanas (poses) or trance dance or lick a gigantic cosmic ice cream cone. You get the idea.

Which form of meditation is the best? The answer is, of course, the one that works for you right now. Explore what you are drawn to, see what resonates most strongly. Many wise people believe that, when in doubt, tools and practices that have been used for thousands of years and that have well-respected, sacred lineages are the ones to pay attention to first. Basically, if they helped all the great spiritual masters experience their inner pots of gold, they can probably help you. But of course, there are no guarantees.

For example, when I first learned to meditate, I tried several traditional techniques for a few years but never experienced much, and it wasn't until I took an esoteric alternative spirituality class that taught a specific energetic technique referred to as "running your energy" that I was able to finally start experiencing what all those thousand-year-old traditions were sighing about. To practice this technique, you concentrate on a detailed visualization of running colored energy through your body in several different directions, and this focused practice quickly helps you enter a calm and meditative space. Now, because of that alternative and some would even say "New Age-y" practice, I'm able to practice traditional techniques more effectively, if I choose. (This is par for the course for me. I've always done things kind of ass backwards.) What I learned, of course, is that it's not always important *how* you connect with divinity, only that you dedicate a certain amount of time, each day, to do it, and only it. Yes, this means discipline, people.

Practice Makes Perfect

Never meditated before? Fear not. Just let go of any preconceived ideas of how you think it's supposed to look or feel, and especially, dump any notions that it takes years to learn how to meditate. What's most important here is your openness and intent.

Some basics: Find a quiet spot where you won't be disturbed. Sit cross-legged on the floor, cushion, or couch, or sit in a chair with your feet flat on the floor. (While you can meditate lying down, for most of us, at least at the beginning, this just turns into a major snooze fest.) Now, either close your eyes, or bring your gaze to a fixed point in the near distance, a few feet down in front of you, and start focusing your attention on your breath. Take a few deep lungfuls, and just become aware of the movement of your breath, slowly, in and out. Notice the sound, the way your lungs and abdomen feel, the way your mind calms and your body relaxes. Do this for a few minutes, maybe more. And there you have it. This is the basic idea. Where you go from here is up to you.

Often incense or essential oils, candles, or calming music (especially ambient-style music with no vocals) can really help set the mood. You might wear special jewelry or hold sacred stones in your hands or meditate under a favorite tree or in front of your personal altar. (See Chapter Five for more on altars.) If you find this basic form too general, you might soon desire a more specific technique, like the Zen no-thought practice mentioned earlier or maybe one of the techniques mentioned below. Your meditation techniques can be passive or active or anywhere in between. This is your practice; the only true rules are your intent and your openness to the experience.

Here's a tiny handful of meditation ideas to give you a taste of the range of techniques you can explore. Try one, try 'em all. And remember, if any really click with you, by all means go a little further and do some research into the practice; look up a meditation center in your town; check out some teachers, books, or related CDs; and go deeper.

• *Receive your self.* When you hear "meditation," you're probably thinking more Buddha than Jesus, right? It's time to change that. Traditionally, Christianity referred to meditation as *contemplation,* which involves thinking about passages from scripture or musing over divine mysteries to generate a deeper understanding and a more loving response. This practice requires deep listening—letting faith grow and allowing answers, directions, deeper meanings to naturally unfold. Jesus didn't teach a specific method but did withdraw regularly to be alone with God. Christian meditation is, therefore, a personal practice of simply being in the presence of the divine, deepening one's loving relationship with God.

Try this: Sit still. Breathe deeply for a few breaths, and then say a word or phrase that means something to you a few times, like "Come, Holy Spirit (or Goddess, or Krishna)," or simply "love," "peace," or "joy." Let this word or phrase fill your heart, your whole body. Or maybe repeat a particularly inspiring line from a favorite spiritual book or poem. Then just listen. Be aware of what sensations, feelings, or insights you may be receiving. If you like, jot 'em down in your red book. Know that you might not feel or hear anything at first; your awareness deepens over time.

• *Say it like you mean it.* As mentioned earlier, Hindus and Buddhists are very fond of using mantras, or *japa,* when they meditate. In this active practice, you repeat a sacred prayer or phrase or names of the divine, over and over again, aloud, until the words become a rhythm and the sound penetrates deep inside your bones. The words and names used in this practice are imbued with tremendous divine power, and it's believed that the very act of saying them invites this sacred energy, this enlightening vibration into your body, your mind, your spirit, even your home, your food, your houseplants. Many people use these mantras as their entire meditation or as a way to begin or end another form of meditation.

Try this: Sit still, and close your eyes. Take a few deep breaths, and chant the simple sound "Om" (the sacred sound from which, according to Hindus and Buddhists, the entire universe was created).

LISTEN

The sound is broken down into three essential parts: A, U and M. When chanted, it sounds like Ahhhhohhhummmmm. Inhale deeply, then exhale the Om for as long as your slow exhalation lasts, expressing the sound in a strong and loud voice that emerges not just from your throat but also from your abdomen and deep in your chest, from your heart center. Pause at the end of the exhalation, then inhale deeply, and begin again. Each Om cycle may take ten, twenty, or even thirty seconds. (If you go longer than this, you may just faint.)

One option: Call around to some yoga studios in your area, and ask if the teacher does any chanting before or after class (many of them do). If so, get in there and Om away.

• *Get golden.* Try this: Place the index finger of one hand just between your eyebrows and about an inch up, aiming inward. Now place the index finger of the other hand just above one ear, aiming in. Imagine two straight lines shooting from those fingers straight through your head. Where those two lines intersect, that's the exact center of your head. Keeping that spot in mind, sit in a chair, spine straight, eyes closed, and take a few deep breaths, relaxing your body. Now imagine a small, luminous golden ball, about the size of a golf ball, spinning slowly, right there in the center of your head. Yep. Smack dab in the middle. Focus your attention, your energy, on this energetic spot, which many spiritual traditions refer to as your third eye. (Have you ever seen Buddhist or Hindu icons or images of deities with three eyes? You're seeing the third eye, the enlightenment button, the sixth chakra.)

This practice quiets your internal dialogue, makes you more neutral, calms the nerves, and stimulates the pituitary gland (which

is considered by spiritual teachers in the East to be the seat of the mind) and the pineal gland (the seat of illumination, intuition, and cosmic consciousness—right on!).

- *Fire works.* There's something about candles. Maybe the dancing flame, the intensely focused heat, the mysterious ambience they evoke. Whatever the reason, a great many people like to meditate by sitting in front of a lit candle, making sure the flame is eye level, and simply staring into the tiny blaze.

Try this: Dim the lights, and sit in a chair or cross-legged on a soft cushion on the floor. Slow down your breath, and really concentrate on the flame, focusing all your attention into the center of the light and allowing any feelings, thoughts, images to emerge naturally and then be let go—or maybe burned up in the flame. See if you can't let your mind be as still as the blue center of the flame—no flickers, no distractions. This sort of intense focus lets the mind begin to unwind, rigid barriers fall, and alternate states of divine communion emerge. What's not to like?

I know, I know. At first, meditation can seem incredibly boring, pointless, or even a little scary, given how most of us have spent our whole lives unconsciously *avoiding* exactly what meditation encourages, which is to be alone—*really* alone—with our selves. Marianne Williamson says that we live in a world that believes if you're not constantly doing something, then you're doing nothing, which somehow translates into the silly idea that *you're* nothing. The irony, Williamson says, is that when we start really practicing "doing nothing" (that is, meditating) in order to cultivate a relationship with our divine spark, we see that we are, in fact, everything. We realize that we are more nurtured through this internal practice than by anything we could do on the outside.

I also know that many may say that meditating just isn't their thing, which is a bit like saying, "Eating healthy works for some people, but it's not really for me." This I can guarantee: *Some* form of meditation or prayer is right for you. Promise. Just be patient with yourself. Try a few techniques; get into the habit of sitting still for just a few minutes a day, expanding to five, ten, twenty, or more. Trust me when I say that even the most practiced meditators out there still experience frustration and boredom and strange little eye tics now and then. No matter. The benefits far outweigh the occasional bouts of frustration and napping. I know, I promised that *The Red Book* will never tell you what to do. I lied. If there's one thing I encourage you to try more than any other in this book, let it be this. Let it be a simple, daily meditation practice. Why? Because essentially, it's the thing that leads to everything else.

Just Be It

Whatever form of meditation or prayer you practice, it should help you attain inner stillness. It should make you more mindful, non-judgmental, and open-hearted. It should help you practice detaching from your mind and ego self, so that the bigger you, the divine spark, your essential nature, can really be felt, can be known, can be experienced. It should root you in the Now and help you learn how to accept what is.

But meditation is only effective if you do it, every day. That's right, every day. Try it early in the morning, just after you wake up. Try it just before bed. It doesn't really matter when. Pick a time

≈ It's Not Always All About You ≈

Becoming quiet and still is also an excellent time to pray for others. In several double-blind studies on distance healing conducted by researchers at Duke and Harvard universities and by the California Pacific Medical Center, the majority of ill people who were prayed for (even when the ill people didn't know anyone was praying for them) healed significantly faster and better than those who were not prayed for.

Buddhist meditation often involves continually sending big doses of compassionate energy to all beings in the universe. One such powerful meditation practice is called *metta*, which means "loving kindness." It's a very simple and direct practice that involves opening your heart to your self, to others, to all of life.

Try this: Imagine someone (or multiple someones) in your life who could use some doses of loving kindness or healing energy. They might be ill, or depressed, or going through a challenging time. Picture them in your mind as you meditate, and simply imagine offering them some love. How? Imagine that love is a color—for example, a shiny, glowing gold. Visualize offering someone in need a ball of this luminous gold as if you were presenting flowers. (Whether the person wants to keep your cool love ball is up to them.) Or bring to your attention the feeling you have when you feel totally and completely loved, and then imagine sharing this feeling with another person or saying, with sincere intention, "I wish you love." And so on. You can do this with strangers, countries, even the entire planet. After all, who couldn't do with more loving kindness?

that's quiet, easy on your schedule, without a lot of distraction. And be aware of becoming overly regimented about how you meditate. I can't tell you how many times I have gotten myself into a rigid practice of meditating in one certain way for exactly so many minutes every day; meanwhile, my spirit was pulling my arm to try something different or to try no technique at all and just relax on my couch with my eyes closed and my heart open. Often, when I just let go of what *should* happen or what I wish would happen or what I think *could* happen, the true magic really starts.

Sometimes when I meditate, I just feel love, or peace, or lightness. Sometimes I feel physical sensations. Sometimes I hear words, but they are not loud or clear and almost seem like I'm imagining them. It's the same with images. But here's the interesting thing: Most of what I receive while meditating is *not* the same as what I see or hear or even feel with my "normal" five senses. I am receiving intuitions (using a sixth sense), and they have a different quality. A softer presence. So soft, in fact, that I've become thankful for the calming and quieting benefits of meditation, because I'm sure I would never experience them otherwise.

Then again, more often than not, I hear, feel, and see absolutely nothing, nada, zippo. This is when I have to fight any urge to try to create something or hear something or imagine something because I think I'm supposed to, and just let myself be. Spiritual teacher Jiddu Krishnamurti said, "Meditation is not a means to an end. It is both the means and the end" (p. 47). I've learned that the least showy of meditation experiences are often the most powerful. Many spiritual teachers will tell you, the favorite language of the divine is silence. When you dedicate time each day to meditation, to giving the divine your full, undivided attention, you are, in essence, learning a new language, a new way of hearing and sensing and feeling. You're realizing that the most intimate, amazing, powerful love affair in the universe is happening right inside your skin.

De-tach

Most of us understand that life is completely transient, constantly evolving and morphing. Seasons, birth and death, random gray hairs—it all feels very *real,* from the ginormous SUVs that screw up our parking karma to the workplace pressures and dramas that screw up our good night's sleep. But as solid and tangible as this world appears, many Eastern philosophies (Hinduism and Buddhism, in particular) believe it's all just a very well maintained *illusion,* all just a series of veils covering the face of Ultimate Reality. While it sure as hell feels very real to our five senses, our divine self, or essential nature—that which we learn to eventually experience during meditation and prayer—is *eternal,* a constant, always calmly chillin' at some metaphysical happy hour; it's aware of but completely unaffected by the churning of the daily world.

This is where the idea of *nonattachment* comes in. This perspective, which we begin to naturally attain through meditation, lets us engage in all our normal worldly activities, but without defining ourselves in terms of them. It's a way of being *in* the world but not *of* it. Nonattachment is the ability to keep our selves free and clear, within the sticky drama of our immediate environment and the mad world violently, beautifully spinning around us. And it covers the whole gamut: from terrorist acts to fights with our sister to the prospect of getting older, from the stress of trying to get that article published to your surprise birthday party to winning the lottery, our sense of self remains steady and complete, no matter what changes our world.

In case you were wondering, detaching in this way doesn't make you an emotionless, uncaring drone. In fact, it can make your life experiences even *more* vivid and emotionally powerful, given how you no longer cling to them or drag them along with you as unnecessary baggage, as heavy, defining inhibition. The world becomes *lighter,* your experiences more pure, less grave and stressful. As real or painful or even joyous as a given drama or emotion may feel, your true power lies in your ability to fully have it, to let it go, and move on.

But Mr. Whiskers <u>Needs</u> Me

Now, the idea that we shouldn't be so desperately attached to external things—like, say, material possessions—is kind of *duh*, because no one really wants to be completely defined by, say, our cars or homes or our new and amazing feather-fringed handbag or what score we get on that grad school exam. But this sort of clear-eyed detachment is merely the first level. When we bring the idea up a notch and practice not being so overly defined by and dependent on, say, our lovers, our family, our friends, our pets, well, things can begin to sound pretty cold.

No doubt, almost everyone on the planet enjoys feeling attached to a group, or a lover, or a family, or a manic, licking feline furball. There's not a thing wrong with this. It feels quite nice. It feels won-

derful and warm. It feels like we're needed and we matter and we belong here. It feels . . . well, it feels like love. But here's the big and sometimes painful-sounding question you must ask about your life: What if all these amazing things went away? What if you lost all the things that surround your life and make it what it is? Would you still have a clear idea of who you are? Would you still feel whole? Would you still feel loved and like you matter? Fact is, many of us wouldn't. Nonattachment doesn't prevent you from feeling pain or from loving all these wonderful things and people and animals, but it *does* help you avoid losing yourself completely within that pain or that love, at the expense of who you really are. It helps you love your loved ones in a way that is more free, that makes you less dependent on them for the feeling of being whole and valid and loved.

Here's another way that meditation can truly help. It's a practice that encourages a loving relationship with your self as a complete spirit, independent of the everyday intrigues of material and emotional life, so that when you really need true love, you first go *in,* before you go *out.* The first person you seek for support and affection and definition of who you are is, well, you. This doesn't mean that you take on some greedy and selfish "me first" ethos, nor will it turn you into some weird hermit chick who hugs herself all day and talks only to plants. It just makes you so full of authentic presence, true love, that you are no longer desperate, clingy, or needy, and therefore you become much more capable of engaging in authentic relationships. Developing a sense of nonattachment makes you a better lover, a better friend, a better daughter, a better sister, a better animal companion, a better *human,* because you have more to give, you are more balanced in how you receive, you are independent and complete with or without someone or something else (sorry, Jerry Maguire, "You complete me" is just not the most spiritually correct thing to say about true love), and this also makes you *very* attractive.

Spiritual Hang-Ups

But that ain't all. Meditation also teaches us how to become less attached to our so-called negative aspects—our fears, jealousies, judgments, abusive tendencies, and disgust with all things polyester, as well as the fact that we have an active and even belligerent ego, a monkey mind, even attachment issues. Nonattachment means that if we notice one of these blemishes on our soul's mirror (or so many that, at first, we can't even see our true reflection), we bravely see it for what it is: a temporary shadow covering the path, even a necessary part of the path, a piece of us that doesn't have to define our entire life.

Oh, and by the way, nonattachment also helps us avoid becoming superglued to the *good* stuff that soothes our souls—all the serendipitous divine winks, warm and fuzzy meditation experiences, humdinger intuitions, and even the extraordinary mystical experiences. Nonattachment helps you realize that those peak moments don't define you, either. Keep the lessons, let go of the experiences. Our inner sense of self should never be overwhelmed by what spiritual lollipops we lick. Practicing nonattachment helps us come to realize that we're simply divine, with or without all the zingy spiritual side effects.

194

Flow Away

Nonattachment might seem slippery and contradictory, but it's not. It simply means taking care not to become super dependent on anything outside of your true self, and that includes spiritual beliefs, or the idea of igniting your divine spark, or meditation. Just as it's vitally important for entire cultures to allow the divine to move, to allow new expressions, and to allow perceptions to change over time, lest that divinity—and that culture—become stagnant (and, possibly, poisonous), so it is for you. Your relationship with the divine should dance and sway, should at all times be dynamic and energized and fluid, constantly redefining itself as you progress. You are always growing, and your consciousness is continuously expanding; so should your relationship to divinity, as well as your expression of it. Attach too strongly to some spiritual practice or definition of the divine that's working for you now, and you could prevent that energy from moving, from evolving, from releasing when it needs to, in order to make room for new awareness, new lessons, new wonder. It's a beautiful inverse relationship: The less clingy and attached you are, the more pure, flowing experience you get to enjoy. Cool, no?

Remember, every concept, every belief has a ceiling, a limit. And we all know that divinity likes to go topless. The trick is to hold certain beliefs that serve you at a particular time but not to cling to them when your spirit wants to become more daring and take it all off. After all, only through your personal change and evolution do those practices have any real effect. This is not to suggest that you should toss away valuable spiritual beliefs whenever you feel the slightest intuitive tug or when you experience a lag; it's just a simple reminder to always be active and open to the new.

All these spiritual techniques and practices are just tools; they are here to help you realize your true divine nature, but they cannot do the work for you. Tools are meant to teach you how to get to a certain point, a point where you can eventually let them go. They can show you the door, but it's up to you, and only you, to walk through.

OPEN *to the new*

CHAPTER 13

Know That You Know
Trusting Your Intuition with Your Life

It's time to flutter your third eye, ignite your sixth sense, and, well, see dead people. And it's time to let go of any preconceived ideas surrounding what you already may believe intuition to be and become more intimate with one of your most powerful, yet severely undervalued natural abilities. After all, the divine is best communicated not mentally, not physically, not even emotionally, but, yes, intuitively (think *internal* divine winks), which makes intuition one of the most important tools for igniting your divine spark, yet often the most difficult to pinpoint and trust. What intuition is: gut hunches, quick flashes of insight, subtle or electric physical sensations, powerful "feelings," visions, that deep and undeniable knowing. What it's not: intellectual mind crunching, crystal-ball gazing, or something utterly mysterious and unholy. In its most basic form, intuition resembles primal (or gut) instinct. In its most exalted form, it's more like full-blown Technicolor mystical visions, almost as real and tangible as the book you hold in your hands right now. For our purposes, we're aiming for somewhere in between.

The Red Book bases much of its philosophy on the fact that you already have this incredibly powerful, internal guidance system, and much of the point of this approach is to encourage you to use this birthright more and more, every day, in nearly everything you do. Paying attention to signs, seeing your life symbolically, interpreting your dreams, peeling your onion, and especially developing a more profound sense of your divine connection via meditation and creative prayer—all of these practices are training you, directly or indirectly, to develop your intuition. So while this chapter focuses specifically on intuition, intuition's many facets inform every chapter of this book.

And while *The Red Book* feels that intuition is incredibly integral to spirituality, how you use it doesn't always have to be quite so, uh, "spiritual." Just as *The Red Book* encourages you to infuse spirituality into every aspect of your life (and reveal to yourself what areas spirituality has always been present in), your intuition, your wise inner guidance, can and should be used for just about anything—from spiritual beliefs to politics, choosing the right new car to wading through the dating pool to deciding whether or not to gulp down that high-fiber vegan chocolate cupcake. Yes, it's that kind of tool. And much like universal divine energy itself, you can only ignore it, acknowledge it in passing (as a "lesser" way of knowing something), or expand its range of power. Guess which one *The Red Book* dives into?

Do You Know What I Know?

Believe it or not, everyone is intuitive. You see, most of us employ our intuitive sense regularly, without even knowing it. It's just an everyday thing. See if you recognize any of these: Intuition is thinking of your friend whom you haven't spoken with in ages, who, shortly thereafter, calls you, out of the blue. Intuition is that fluttering feeling in your belly, telling you not to walk down that street this particular night. It's a blushing sense of pulsing familiarity when you meet someone new. It's a subtle sense that you should come in to the office early or not give that guy your number, purchase that used computer, or agree to take on a new project that, for some reason, doesn't sit right with you. (In popular movies and in fiction, intuition takes the form of people who suddenly decide, for no apparent reason, as they're walking down the jetway, not to get on that flight after all—and sure enough, the plane later takes a nosedive). Intuition is suddenly knowing just the right words to say to your distraught sister, the best way to confront an aggressive colleague, or the healthiest decision to make for yourself, right now. Mystic Ron Roth says that intuition is "how you know that you know that you know," but you don't exactly know why or how you know.

Unfortunately, not everyone pays attention to their intuition or acts on the insights they receive. Intuitive ignorance is epidemic, as most of us were not raised in a society or a culture that encourages or supports this less reasonable, less "normal," less *obvious* way of knowing. Many people don't trust the intangible, especially when it's based on personal experience.

Why? Well, there are many theories. Perhaps Plato's objectification of ideas, or dogmatized, demystified, institutionalized belief systems, or the scientific method, the industrial revolution, the birth of the rationalists, the subjugation of the divine feminine, a great cosmic fog of forgetfulness, and many other things have helped create a world in which sensing is buried in favor of strict logic. Ironically, today, the best scientists and lawyers and detectives and think tank researchers and inventors are usually quite intuitive. They go with their gut. They just have a certain sense about something, so they follow through; they just don't always tell others about their original knowing. Einstein stated, "The intellect has little to do on the road to discovery. There comes a leap in consciousness, call it intuition or what you will, and the solution comes to you and you don't know how or why." Problems arise when we lose our ability to sense for ourselves what is right for us or not, when we usurp our own knowing in favor of an external rule or law or method. Although much of this world rides high on rationality, reason, concrete examples, and proof—things that make most intuitive hunches want to hide more than seek—it's time to stop hiding.

Imagine All the People

If you're up for a little intuitive experiment, try this exercise. Next time you're about to go into a party or a restaurant or hop a ride on the subway, stop and take a minute to calm your mind, focus on your breath, and relax your body. Then, once you go in, try to shift your attention away from your basic sensory input, like how someone looks or smells, and pay attention to how a person *resonates* with you, how they make you feel on a deeper level, physically, mentally, emotionally, and, yep, energetically. Check out how your body responds. Does it grow warm or cold or feel ill? Do you immediately get jumpy or calm or feel pain or fatigue? What about the emotional response? Do you start to feel happy or sad, depressed or defensive, or even giddy?

In other words, see who, just by their very presence, makes you light up and smile and who sort of weighs you down or sucks you dry. Does any sort of image or color, song or word pop up in the back of your mind or on the tip of your tongue when someone first comes into your presence? Take note of what you're sensing—even if you think you're just imagining it, even if you think your brain is just

⇒ I Can Feel You Looking at Me ⇐

According to Rupert Sheldrake, a biochemist and author of the intriguing book *The Sense of Being Stared At*, unexplained human abilities such as telepathy, the sense that someone is looking at you, and premonition (among others) are not the slightest bit woo-woo paranormal but rather are absolutely normal, part of our biological nature. Sheldrake studied and performed numerous experiments in which humans demonstrated, without fail, that they sense with more than the basic five senses.

Some of his research demonstrated how we are all able to pick up others' thoughts and intentions, even when the people are in a different room or on the telephone with us. And that most of us sense when we are being stared at, even when the person doing the staring is not in our line of sight. Sheldrake also researched several mothers and their ability to know when their children are in trouble without communication through normal means (mail, e-mail, phone), even when the children live across the country or even across the world. This ability has been referred to as "women's intuition" by the mainstream or "that freaking crazy extraordinary mom sense. . . . I mean, how does she *know* I'm sleeping with Keith again?" by spooked and frustrated children.

playing around, dredging up funny pictures to amuse you because you told it to. In fact, tuning in to your imagination in this way is one of the fastest roads to becoming more intuitive.

With this (or any) intuitive exercise, don't try too hard or restrict yourself. Humor is key. Have fun, and if you want, track your impressions in your own red book. You might be surprised, when you come back to it later, at how right on you were in hearing, somewhere in the back of your head, the Stones' "Sympathy for the Devil" when you first saw that waiter. You can do this type of intuitive experimenting anywhere and with anyone or anything—from spiritual books to medicine to picking out running shoes. It's that kind of tool. No limits, no restrictions.

That's Not a Bestseller with Me

In fact, this sort of exercise is perfect when you're investigating the huge, convoluted world of spirituality. Pay close attention as you work your way around: Does that class, book, practice, teacher, or tradition make you feel a little heavy, stressed, or depressed or make your body feel slightly nauseous or headachy? Chances are that it's not resonating positively with you and that you should probably drop it for now, even if it's supposedly reputable or time-honored or "serious," or even if it's a big splashy *New York Times* bestseller with gobs of celebrity endorsements, or even if your best friend absolutely *swears* it changed her life and the lives of absolutely everybody she knows, including her dog. Doesn't matter. Trust your gut.

Conversely, if that material warms you to your core, opens your heart, makes your body tingle, sparks your mind—if it just *feels good in your hands*—then cool; this is obviously a positive resonation. Try it out for a while. But be aware of appearances. Keep in mind, resonation is not just a cute marketing agenda, a "My favorite Hindu deity is on that hip poster for the 10 Days to Enlightenment Workshop, so it must be good," nor is it your ego's voice; it's a conscious and *intuitive* awareness, a deep knowing that comes from inside you, not outside you.

You'd be amazed how many people stick with something spiritual, even though it doesn't truly resonate with them ("My partner really gets something out of this tradition, so I'm sure I will too . . . someday"), or reject something that does resonate, because it's not what they *think* they should be into ("Working with crystals? No way. I'm a devout anti–New Ager"). Your divine spark has more important things to do than match your personal preferences and appease your ego. It resonates with what will help make you whole, what will help you grow deeper In Love. Developing your resonance skills takes a little time and practice, lots of "Oh, so that was my intuition telling me to avoid that workshop, not just my acid reflux." But just being aware of this dynamic while you explore spirituality is a good start. I know that if I had been encouraged to pay more attention to resonation when I was first exploring spirituality, I would have saved myself a lot of time, money, and confusion, not to mention a great deal of personal power.

Dare to Know

Using our intuition also allows us to feel out certain beliefs, and sense whether they align with us or not, free of the dictates of ex-

ternal authority. It works for everything: Political, social, cultural, economic, spiritual, scientific, nutritional, medical, and media-driven beliefs are always ripe for pruning. You're receiving intuitive guidance about all of them, all the time, but if you don't take the time to become familiar with how your inner self communicates with you, then you could end up blindly accepting what I say or what Guru Whatshername chants in that workshop or what the president mumbles or what the FDA claims. And that's not very empowering—in fact, it's kind of lazy. The Buddha said, "Believe nothing, no matter where you read it, or who said it, no matter if I have said it, unless it agrees with your own reason and your own common sense." Gandhi put it this way: "Even as wisdom comes from the mouth of a babe, so does it often come from the mouths of old people. The golden rule is to test everything in light of reason and experience, no matter from where it comes."

Here's a potent modern example: When Pope Benedict trudges out to declare, once again, that homosexuality is morally evil, and if you're just not quite sure what to believe, simply check in with yourself. Don't merely analyze the data, listen to arguments from liberals or conservatives, scour the Bible for some sort of mistranslated or misinterpreted proof that God said homosexuality is a sin, or fall back on past prejudices or fears. Simply get quiet, clear your mind, and sit with this idea. Pay attention to any and every sensation. What does your heart say when you think about homosexuality being morally evil? What does your spirit whisper? How does your body feel?

Here's an even harsher example: Let's say that your doctor says you have cancer and you have, at best, only five more years left to live. He is basing his judgment on statistics and all sorts of tests and science and so on and so forth. (Not that any of these sources are necessarily bad, but remember, your spirit is not limited to or threatened by statistical reality.) Now, you have two choices: You can accept your doctor's belief as absolute truth and let his diagnosis become a permanent part of your reality, or you can say, "Thank you very much, good doctor, but I'm getting a second opinion. My own."

I know, it sounds like scientific blasphemy, and you might be thinking you have no right to disrespect the medical or scientific (or even cancer survivor) communities this way. But if you try listening to what your spirit says about whatever dis-ease shows up in your life, you may hear a rather different opinion than the one the medical profession can offer. You may come to realize that healing this dis-ease will not depend on anything outside of yourself. Or you may feel that it's best to do a "both and" approach instead of an "either or," and add alternative medicine to whatever treatment your doctor prescribes. In other words, it's very likely that your intuition may lead you to a whole range of medicines, healers, relationships, exercises, foods, or even roller skates to try (stuff not only that your doctor isn't trained to know much about and has no financial incentive to encourage but about which he has no real authority to sway you, one way or the other).

Listen to your intuition and you may hear, for example, that you need to truly forgive your father for divorcing your mother when you were young. You may be led to an intense meditation practice, a strange-sounding water therapy treatment, or a unique teacher who can help guide you to a place of peace, *despite* your previous intense fear of death, and therefore help you gain a loving acceptance of what is—thus receiving a true healing, even if you're not "cured." It's impossible for me to guess how and where your intuition will guide you. I can only promise that if you really learn to listen to that most personal and sacred inner voice, it will.

Help, I Think My Intuition Is Broken

You say you've tried the people-gauging exercise and the belief-testing exercise, maybe many times over, but you still just can't sense a damn thing? Don't worry. Your intuition is like a muscle; it takes time to develop, and in many cases, our intuition has been buried under so many thick layers of logic and doubt and misinformation that the muscle might take a little coaxing to make itself known. My point is, we've all got the intuitive muscle, but most of us have to really exercise in order to experience its strength and support. And, while some of us may be inclined to work out till we're intuitive power lifters, whereas others of us might just want to keep our intuition toned and flexible, none of us should let that muscle atrophy and get flabby and weak. And just as swimming does my best friend's body good, while cycling works for my sister and yoga for my boyfriend, we all have to find what intuitive exercises fit our individual lifestyles and personalities and spiritual goals.

What's more, the simple exercises that I suggest in this chapter only scratch the surface, and they may not be the best for your particular strength of instinct. When it comes to subtle messages from the universe within and outside, some of us are better at seeing (clairvoyance), some of us are better at hearing (clairaudience), some better at sensing (clairsentience), some better at knowing (clairgnosis), and some of us are just better at doing nothing but keeping ourselves conscious and open, so when we do feel a particular tingle while walking through the park, we pay attention.

There are countless excellent books and workshops that can teach you various ways to develop your intuition. Some of these work to accelerate your psychic abilities (that is, the ability to observe someone's past lives or energy body or to check in with this or that dimensional being or to experience fancy astral projections, and so on). All well and good, but being psychic is not at all necessary when it comes to igniting your divine spark. (Using your intuition is not necessarily being psychic, but being psychic is a way of using intuition.)

In fact, many spiritual teachers see our modern fascination with psychic powers as a distraction, as a desire for cheap party favors or unconscious ways in which we try to control life, predict our future, keep ourselves safe. They believe that if we spend most of our time trying to become psychic, we're missing the juicy divine point. In fact, if we all just spent more time being our divine selves, here and now, we'd probably, very organically, start becoming more psychic anyway. It's a matter of priorities, I guess. So while I do believe that becoming more aware of your innate intuitive abilities and allowing them more prominence in your daily life is incredibly important, learning how to intuit the next card in a blackjack game or "reading" what's to come in your next love relationship is not. (Although the former *would* make a trip to Vegas a lot more interesting. . . .)

Again, I believe that one of the best ways to develop your intuition is simply to meditate. Regularly. As I laid out in Chapter

Twelve, when we learn to pipe down and calm the mind, we become more and more familiar with the way our divine spark communicates with us. Meditation and creative prayer let us give this inner voice—our intuition—the attention it needs to grow and strengthen, so we become better at hearing our divine selves not only when we're sitting pretty but also right during the muck and muddle of our daily lives.

Read Me

Once in a while—ah, sweet paradox—when my abilities to hear my divine spark feel gummed up and stuck, I go visit an alternative

⇒ Shhhhhh . . . ⇒

In 1995, the U.S. government (particularly the CIA and the DIA) finally admitted to the media that they had been using psychics for the past twenty years in attempts to hunt down Libyan leader Muammar al-Qaddafi, find plutonium in North Korea, and help drug enforcement agencies track down smugglers, among other things. These psychic studies were supposedly called "Project Stargate," which is just so phenomenally 1975. But even today, it's commonly known that military and government leaders and even local police forces will often employ a psychic (or "intuitive reader") to help figure out enemy tactics or solve various crimes. They just don't like to talk about it much.

therapist and get myself an intuitive reading. That's right, I go see what some would label a "psychic" (though my definition is far different than what you might normally associate with this word; see the next box). Now, I firmly believe, based on my own experience, that with the unstoppable combo of clear intention, meditation and prayer, and being open to signs and letting go of tension, the confusion will eventually dispel. Even so, sometimes a really ethical, grounded, compassionate intuitive reading can help me shift a bit easier and faster.

Astrologers, tarot readers, energy workers, spiritual healers, neo-shamans, genuine palm readers—all of these can offer profound clues to your unique makeup. More often than not, true intuitive readers won't tell you anything that you don't already know, deep down, in your heart of hearts, but they might highlight issues about which you might not have trusted your own intuition just yet or that you might not yet want to admit. Sometimes it's intensely effective to hear this "nothing new" from a stranger, presented to you in a way or with a perspective that you hadn't thought of before. For those of us who are getting accustomed to using our intuition, a skilled intuitive can sometimes provide a sort of cross-check, a reminder, or even a lesson that teaches us to pay closer attention to ourselves.

But as always, be aware. Be careful. Just because someone is psychic or can sense energy fields or can hear your guardian angels, that doesn't mean that all the information they are giving is right for you. Gauge carefully. After a reading, you should feel empowered and enabled, not needy and dependent. And know that whatever is said is not set in stone. Usually information is given to us at a

⇒ And He Will Be Tall, Dark, ⇐ and Handsome

From psychics to palm readers to energy healers, you've gotta sort through a lot of bullshit, separate the Miss Cleos from the Caroline Mysses in order to really benefit. What to look for when engaging intuitive practitioners: ethics; compassion; helpful, grounded information; encouragement to trust your inner knowing and find your own answers; and a clear respect for your boundaries. What to beware of: future forecasts, fear-based or highly confusing information, pointed advice, and "special services" offered to you for an extra cost.

Authentic readers simply give you insight into your current situation, tell you where your energies lie, where they might be stuck, and maybe advise you on honing and redirecting those energies toward your goals. Basically, they help install some streetlights on your path, so that you can see where the hell you are and where you might be headed.

particular time in order to spark us in a new direction or to encourage us to get our butt in gear and make some healthy changes. Remember, your greatest gift is your freedom of choice. You are *always* free to determine a new course for your life.

And by the way, being psychic does not necessarily mean that someone is more spiritually advanced. It just means that they've developed their antennae to such a degree that they can tune in to more subtle frequencies; it doesn't mean that they've mastered the art of *translating* those frequencies. If you're not careful, you can end up substituting an intuitive's knowing for your own knowing or begin to trust what they see over what you feel, and the reading will just distract you and send you into an unhealthy tailspin. So if you're interested in seeing an intuitive, be extremely discerning and selective. Don't go just because you're too lazy to really listen for your own answers or because you're lonely and you just want to know whether your tall, dark, and handsome is coming around the next corner, and for another 100 bucks, exactly which corner.

This Is Not a Whim

While intuitive practice can be quite helpful, don't ever put pressure on yourself to "be intuitive." You don't have to do anything unnatural. In fact, many people realize that they followed their intuition only *after* the fact. They felt like turning right instead of left, so they did. They didn't stop in the middle of the road and interrupt the natural flow with questions.

Here's an example of going with the flow despite some initial hesitation. One weekend I walked into a great used bookstore in Berkeley with the idea of buying a certain fiction book by a renowned author. But just as I started browsing the fiction aisle, I was immediately drawn to an unfamiliar book by an author I had never heard of. Against my intellect ("Why *that* random book? You came here for some award-winning literature"), I decided, on a "whim," to purchase the strange book, not quite knowing what it was about. As it turned out, the story took place in a mythic ancient Chinese kingdom, where a group of unique and talented young women developed a powerful sisterhood through a traditional female practice called *Jin-shei*. When you ask someone to be your *Jin-shei bao*, and she agrees, you become "heart sisters" for life, meaning that you agree to love each other and support each other, no matter what. Your link is stronger than family or lovers or even hormones. And any other *Jin-shei baos* you or your heart sister acquire then become *Jin-shei baos* with each other, and so the web of powerful sisterhood grows.

Now, I know this sounds a bit like 1980s friendship bracelets, but the touching story greatly inspired me at that particular time. See, my own dear friend was about to move from her beloved San Francisco to New York City, and the small women's group she had started (and of which I was a happy part) was heartbroken to lose her. For our last meeting, we had all agreed to bring something to represent a farewell—and now, because of that book, I knew just what to do. My coast-hopping friend bought us all red Urban Outfitters T-shirts featuring Superwoman and the words "Ladies Night" (which is how we referred to our women's group). Another in the group gave us all beautiful little red silk satchels with good luck tokens from Santa Fe inside, and another had us perform an amazing basil leaf–burning ritual. My ritual was, of course, for each of us to write *Jin-shei* on fine red paper and pass them around, promising we would be heart sisters forever (and now we had the perfect red satchels to hold the red notes). When I told my friends about the meaning of *Jin-shei,* they all got tears in their eyes and just nodded. Later, I found out that they told other girlfriends who were similarly affected. And the meaning spread (as did our fun with saying "*Jin-shei!*"

really fast, with a variety of quirky comic accents, whenever we were talking about something feminine and powerful).

Of course, I realize now why that book jumped out at me. It had a particularly poignant message not only for me but also for those around me. Sort of random. Sort of not. The point is, back in that bookstore, I was being intuitive without really trying, without even knowing it. The universe was winking, and all I had to do was shut off my logical brain (and drop the expectations that I had had when I entered the store) and follow through. It's a very simple example, but the basic lesson applies to just about everything in your life.

Being intuitive is not about trying real hard, it's about relaxing real soft. It's not a mind game or an act of sheer willpower. Like a cell phone in the mountains, your perfectionist ego will simply not work in your spirit's domain. It's simply out of range. In fact, it's not so much about learning how to be intuitive as it's about *unlearning* everything you've been taught that has made you believe you could never have a gift this powerful.

Mission Possible

Then there are those times when you receive such an outlandish intuitive zap that you seriously consider dumping this spiritual stuff altogether and just popping some good quality meds like everyone else and zoning out in front of the TV for a month. It can happen. Maybe one fine day you'll be sweating hard on the treadmill, when *boom,* from outta nowhere you suddenly "get" an idea to quit your job and move to Turkey and study rug making. Say what? How bizarro random is that? You try to shake it off, blame it on dehydration and the three Luna bars you had for breakfast, but the days and weeks pass, and the weird intuition keeps bubbling up from somewhere deep inside you. So what's going on here?

These are what *The Red Book* refers to as "lightning-bolt intuitions"; when a metaphorical Zeus royally scorches your booty so dramatically, you have trouble sitting down in the same place afterward. These spiritual shocks are indeed wake-up calls from the universe, and they are a particularly loud opportunity for you to practice trusting the unknown.

You, as always, have a choice. You can do what most people do, which is ignore this not-so-subtle Turkish intuition and go about your life, with some slight question always nagging at you, or you can choose to give the idea a little room to expand, no matter how insane it seems ("Leave my friends, my job, my life? I don't even speak Turkish!"). Sit with the idea consciously, and if you're still getting a "Yes, go, do it," then, oh, I dunno, *trust it* and get your ass to Turkey. Again, your divine spark is not interested in making you miserable. It's not gonna screw you over and leave you wandering Istanbul penniless and friendless and suffering from a nasty wool allergy. When your intuition comes on that strong, you can be confident in the fact that there is *something* your spirit wants you to discover.

A new career? A talent for learning Turkish? A love relationship you could never have predicted otherwise? Perhaps. Or maybe it's simply a new open attitude toward life, toward yourself, toward others? Or something even more intangible yet no less rewarding, like the realization that no matter what shows or does not show up

215

for you in Turkey, you get to experience the powerfully giddy feeling of what it's like to dance through this world based on internal divine guidance, not just external social prescriptions. Yep, moving to Turkey might just be the best way for you, at this point in your life, to witness another facet of your sparkling potential. There is, of course, only one way to find out.

As Caroline Myss and many other wise teachers frequently point out, when you receive a lightning-bolt intuitive hit about a new direction to take in your life, it's often for something you have no skills in whatsoever, something that takes you outside your normal range of experience and far away from your comfort zone. Make a film when you've only ever been a cine-fan. Open a school for girls in India when you've barely made it past high school yourself. Start your own business when you've only ever been an ordinary cube slave. Propose a cleaner air initiative to your local government when you don't even know what chlorofluorocarbon is. I'm here to attest, the divine often has some stranger than strange–sounding ideas, and your intuition is its favorite messenger.

The real question is, will you courageously follow your own lead, no matter how crazy it might seem? Because "impossible" is not a part of your spirit's vocabulary. The divine will never lead you over a cliff without providing a trampoline down below, even if it appears, from your current vantage point, like stone-cold cement. Eileen Caddy, an American astronaut and the first woman to command a space shuttle mission, gives this advice: "Live by intuition and inspiration and let your whole life be Revelation." Remember, you are not here to play it safe. You are here to start fires.

Role Playing

As you've probably gathered by now, you have a special purpose. You've got certain things to do and people to see and flowers to smell and experiences to have that your intuition is constantly guiding you toward. You have a role that needs to be played, and chances are, it's the role of a lifetime. When lived truthfully, this role will consist of doing and being what you love *and* making a decent living from it. Whoa. Imagine that.

Now before you start dreaming of exotic travels and radical business plans and living in Turkey, please realize that most people's roles while here on this earthly plane for such a quick blink of time aren't nearly so dramatic or far-reaching; one person's role might be as seemingly simple as becoming, say, a conductor of high-frequency love while living on a particularly bleak city block, while another's is to be an amazing mother, while another's is to grow organic food, or save lemurs, or work at that magazine.

Although your intuition might lead you (or might have already led you) toward a role that might not seem all that glamorous, it doesn't make it any less important or meaningful or soul-rocking. There might be thousands of first-grade teachers, but only you can give hope to those specific children in that specific school at that specific time. Let's face it, not everyone can be a Nelson Mandela, because as amazing as that man is, the universe doesn't need millions of him. The universe needs, well, you. And only you can do what it is you do, in your unique way. So please don't shut down your unique abilities with doubt or comparisons or critiques

SPIRITUAL *Superstar*

("Working at this café or teaching music to the elderly or writing poetry on my lunch break can't be all that cosmically significant; just look at that guy I saw on *20/20* who's setting up HIV clinics in Africa"). Gandhi said, "Whatever you do may seem insignificant to you, but it is most important that you do it." Trust me, when you believe in yourself and fulfill your role to the best of your ability, you are a spiritual superstar, as powerful and as needed as any soul on the planet. As modern dance genius Martha Graham so beautifully put it, "There is a vitality, a life force, a quickening that is translated through you into action. And because there is only one of you in all time, this expression is unique. And if you block it, it will never exist through any other medium and be lost. The world will not have it. It is not your business to determine how good it is: nor how it compares with other expressions. It is your business to keep it yours, clearly and directly. To keep the channel open" (quoted in Rob Brezsny's *Pronoia,* p. 76).

This is a mysteriously connected universe. We don't always consciously know how far our energy might reach and how intense its effect might be, but by doing what you intuitively feel you should be doing in this world (be it a career, a project, an art piece, a relationship), you are actually, believe it or not, helping to infuse this planet and even the entire cosmos with deep soulful purpose as well as encouraging other beings to seek out and bravely live their own role. (There is more about this phenomenon in the next chapter.)

Of course, when we start becoming more connected to and more expressive of who we really are, the seemingly random roles we play become just natural extensions of ourselves. Intuitive hits

218

about what your role is (for right now) may not always suggest a huge change from what you are already doing, but they should help you do what you do more consciously. Richard Bach wrote, "Here is a test to find whether your mission on earth is finished: if you're alive, it isn't" (*Illusions,* p. 159). So what's *your* part to play now? How can you be it even better? Don't know if you've found what you're meant to do or be quite yet? Don't fret; when it's time, the universe will give you plenty of external and internal hints, but here's mine: You'll know when you find it because it will make you feel very alive, happy, aligned, content—even if it challenges you and pushes your limits and freaks you out a bit. You will know, on a cell-tingling level, that you are doing what you are meant to do, no matter how mundane it might appear to others, or even to your ego. You will know by how intensely you're existing.

CHAPTER 14

Keep Your Self Buzzing
Crank Your Vibe;
It's Your Cosmic Duty

Of course, you know that you (literally) vibrate, right? Did you know that you can control that vibe? Recognize it in others? Feel it everywhere and anywhere? You can. Energy is in. Energy is where it's at. Energy is the new black of the spiritual season, and for amazingly good and integral reasons—just ask any quantum physicist or Hindu saddhu (holy man).

The relatively new and fascinating field of quantum physics is dramatically changing the scientific landscape, proving that everything in this world and the universe really is connected. First, quantum physics has found that while this world appears solid, all matter, at the subatomic level, is made up of a whole lotta nothing, more space than substance, a few particles whirling in a space vacuum. The basis of reality is ambiguously fuzzy. How reassuring! What's more, physicists have found that when two objects collide and then stop interacting, they remain, at this same subatomic, energetic level, connected. They "stick" to each other in some truly magical and astounding ways. Following a collision, these objects are never truly separate again, even though they might be far apart from each other—so that when one changes, so does the other. Instantly. Faster than the speed of light (sorry, Einstein). This energetic connection is called *quantum interconnectedness*. And given how we all emanate from the same original cosmic space dust and given how subatomic collisions are happening all the time, well, science now says we're probably connected to even the most distant part of the universe.

Quantum physicists tell us that this notion of instant inter-connectedness also implies that space is, well, an illusion, as is time, and that the distance between sources of energy means nothing and has little or no effect on their behavior. (No doubt, this is part of the reason why distance healing and prayers are proving to be so successful.) It's all just a little mind-boggling, but for our purposes, this is the takeaway: Nothing is as solid is as it seems, and we have an energetic reach far wider than ever was scientifically expected or imagined in the past.

Now, here's the intriguing thing. All this quantum jingle sounds awfully similar to a tune that many spiritual traditions have whistled over the centuries. Case in point: the Vedantic branch of Hindu phi-losophy, which believes this world is indeed an illusion *(maya)* and that the only true and constant thing is conscious divine energy, which pervades all. Because everything is essentially made up of this mysterious divine energy, All is One, all is interconnected, despite any illusions we hold about being separate. We are all simply indi-vidual fingers of the same hand. Buddhism has a similar belief, sometimes referred to as *anatman,* that all things are interconnected and interdependent. No thing—including ourselves–has a truly separate existence. It's always intriguing when science finally starts catching up with the mystical.

Because we're all connected to (and emerge from) the same energy source, what happens to me essentially happens to everyone on some very subtle level. What happens to that Muslim woman in Iraq is, on some level, happening to us all. This is our shared humanity, the idea that none of us exists separate and distinct from everyone else. So on an everyday level, when you're nasty to someone else (or even to yourself), not only does your nastiness affect those around you, but that negative energy feeds into the entire universe, like a drop of black water in a blue sea. Our actions, our prayers, our emotions, our thoughts, all have universal implications. (By the way, this is yet another reason why calming your mind via meditation is so helpful.)

This is why all the great traditions espouse some variation of what Jesus so famously taught: "Do unto others as you would have them do unto you," and "Love your neighbor as yourself." Jesus wasn't just being sweet and nice;—he was telling it like it is, on an energetic level, by asking us to step up to the plate and be more responsible for the vibes we give off.

You Must Play with Puppies

The mystics know it, and science proves it: *Everything* in this universe vibrates at a particular frequency, and we, as energetic beings, are constantly picking up these other frequencies and allowing them to change and affect our own. For example, love has a lighter, faster energy than fear, which has a denser, slower energy. (You can probably simply feel this to be true.) Giggling with your baby niece speeds you up, while watching yet another murder on the nightly news slows you waaaaay doooown.

Again, this is where meditation comes in, helping you tune in, raise your antenna, and make yourself more receptive to higher

≋ Serving Others ≋

Gandhi "got" the buzz. He said, "Consciously or unconsciously, every one of us does render some service or another. If we cultivate the habit of doing this service deliberately, our desire for service will steadily grow stronger, and it will make not only for our own happiness, but that of the world at large."

Yep, you guessed it. A great way to raise the planetary vibe is to get out and help others. When we give of ourselves to others—volunteering at a homeless shelter, the Humane Society, or a retirement center, or even simply paying for the next car at the toll plaza or planting trees in a treeless part of the city or smiling more often at bank tellers—our immune systems surge, endorphins crank, hearts open, and the vibe is higher not only for those you help but even for those who witness or hear about your generosity. Gandhi also said, "To give pleasure to a single heart by a single act is better than a thousand heads bowing in prayer." An excellent book that discusses this sort of action through hundreds of moving and deeply inspiring examples is Caroline Myss's *Invisible Acts of Power*. Now, go put a daisy on a stranger's windshield.

frequencies and more capable of deflecting the slower. Want to sustain low, unhealthy vibrations? Be cynical, angry, rant about the world, bitch and complain and stress and wallow and wish others ill and flip off other drivers on the freeway. Want to tap into and sustain a (literally) higher vibration, one that promotes health and joy and intergalactic love cookies? Meditate, pray creatively, read uplifting books, watch heartwarming movies, have more good sex (become friendly with the fast-vibrating goddess, the Hitachi Magic Wand), shake your booty, laugh, offer up huge doses of compassion, give generously to others, and generally refuse to entertain the world's (or even just your colleague's or your lover's or that other driver's) negative energies in your space. And of course, always, play with slobbery, pudgy puppies.

Force of Life

Although it might seem as though every spiritual teacher and book is trumpeting the energy message these days, don't think it's a new phenomenon. Energy has been honored and defined as the foundation of us all, as the power that unites and animates, by every spiritual tradition, from time immemorial. Eastern religions sometimes call it *chi* or life force, while Hinduism calls it *prana*. The Lakota Sioux call it *niyan;* Judaism sometimes refers to it as *rueh;* Muslims call it *barraka*. In Hawaiian, it is called *ti* or *ki*. In fact, the true Aramaic word for "God" is *Alaha,* a name used by Jews of Jesus' time that means "essence" or "substance of all being" but originally meant "breath" and "life force." So when Jews prayed to God, they were actually communicating with the energy of all creation. Every breath was an inhalation of divine presence.

In Eastern medicine, when a person's *chi* or *prana* is low, he or she is more vulnerable to physical, mental, and spiritual dis-ease. A patient is encouraged to consume foods with a lot of inherent life force (natural, whole foods), drink pure water, get lots of fresh

☞ Say Thank You ☞

Here's a simple exercise to help you raise your vibe, popularized by author Sarah Ban Breathnach in her book *Simple Abundance.* Say thank you. For everything. As thirteenth-century German mystic Meister Eckhart wrote, "If the only prayer you said in your whole life was 'thank you,' that would suffice."

One way to cultivate this attitude of gratitude is to write down five things you are grateful for in your red book each day. Make it a daily thanksgiving. The things you are thankful for need not be profound or enormous. You could be grateful for the simplest things: the sun was out today, I had my favorite cereal this morning, the clear silence I experience when I swim under water, clean sheets, irony, the way he looked at me during lunch, Nietzsche, my cool goldfish, music, having a dishwasher, the smell of lavender, my parents' support, foot massages, sand in my hair, free trade coffee, neofeminism, my best friend's sense of humor, my sister's hand-me-down jeans, purple nail polish, dreams of flying, screenwriter Charlie Kaufman, the moment when my boss gave me the thumbs-up sign, the stranger who held the elevator door for me.

You'll be amazed at how many things you can come up with to be thankful for every day of your life and at how simply acknowledging these simple things can make you feel better. After all, gratitude is one of the highest and most important vibrations you can hold in this universe.

air and natural light, and cultivate some sort of practice that helps raise and maintain energetic stamina. Eastern doctors (and now, even some Western docs are finally catching on) might also encourage specific healing treatments and modalities that would directly affect the person's energy system, like acupuncture or *tai chi*, which help keep the life force pumping strong. Modern energy workers are able to sense a person's life force and help smooth out any bumps (during a reading, most good intuitives are simply reading the client's energy body) so that she can flow more freely and fabulously.

So take some time to learn what affects your *chi*—what powers your life force and what drains it. See if you can start sensing that force all around you—in trees, in other people, in that organic apple from the grocery store. Be open to this timeless way of perceiving the inner and outer world, and of course, don't forget to breathe more deeply, love more freely, and think more positively. After all, it's your cosmic duty.

⇒ Water Your Self ⇐

Have you heard of the book *The Message from Water,* which documents the fascinating research of Japan's Masaru Emoto? The book is full of ultra-close-up photographs of water crystals, taken when the water is in its natural state and then again after the water has been kept in various containers on which were written words such as "love" or "peace" or "thank you." Astoundingly, over a short period of time, the crystals begin to change from their basic lumpy, nondescript shape and form breathtakingly beautiful snowflake-like patterns. Conversely, water held in containers that had the words "hate" or "war" or "jealousy" written on them soon looked fractured and damaged and smashed, as if the snowflake had been exploded or ruined. The effect was startling. Any negative energy (even thoughts and intentions) aimed at the water soon turned the crystals into mutated shards. The results of Emoto's studies have struck a chord in many people around the world, resulting in a lot of Nalgene water bottles scripted with "love and gratitude" in yoga classes. More important, Emoto's water studies lead us to watch our thoughts toward each other and ourselves, especially when you realize that the human body is made up of *70 percent water.* You just gotta ask yourself, What sort of messages am I giving to others and myself every day? Am I producing beautiful cellular snowflakes, or stomping on them?

FABULOUSLY

CHAPTER 15

The Joke's on Us
The One Mandatory Ingredient for Every Path

A dear friend once told me this very red little story: During a particularly intense meditation retreat, a woman broke down in tears while sharing an utterly tragic, heart-wrenching personal tale with the wise teacher. The Buddhist master listened to her sobs and gently offered her several helpful perspectives from which to view her circumstances, talking to her for a good half hour in soothing tones. But all of a sudden, the wise master stopped with the gentle wisdom, paused, and said something like, "Or everything I just said might be complete bullshit." And then his body started shaking. My friend realized that this prominent and very wise Buddhist teacher, who, moments before, had been counseling a deeply troubled woman, was heaving with laughter. My friend was stunned. Her first reaction was to be shocked and even a little offended (I mean, that woman was *seriously* sobbing!), but then something odd happened. My friend quickly became infected with the master's buoyant energy, and she started giggling herself, and pretty soon, once everyone got by their initial shock, the whole room, including the previously pained woman, was howling with laughter.

Countless are the wise masters who've said that our entire existence, as meaningful and profound as it is, is also probably one big cosmic joke. On us. Legendary comic Charlie Chaplin once said, "In the end, everything is a gag." Take a look around your life sometime; it can certainly *feel* like life is one giant prank. We've all had those surreal moments (that Buddhist teacher was definitely feeling one), like when you're staring down some seriously lofty truths or reeling from some profound personal realizations or listening, reading, or speaking about something so incredibly deep and heavy it would make flowers cry, and then you get this sort of weird existential hiccup. Your lens shifts, your spiritual underpants are pulled down, and some raw part of you is suddenly exposed. The world, you, all of us wrapped up in our super-serious "spirituality," all suddenly appear to be like cute, tiny frozen peas, packed away in the back freezer aisle of the universe's supermarket of possibilities. It hits you like a rubber chicken smacked across your skull: We've only just *begun* to realize who we are and what this place is made of, and even when we do, we still could be, well, totally wrong.

The author of *The Hitchhikers Guide to the Galaxy*, the late, great Douglas Adams, wrote, "There is a theory which states that if ever anyone discovers exactly what the Universe is for and why it is here, it will instantly disappear and be replaced by something even more bizarre and inexplicable. There is another theory which states that this has already happened" (Prologue, *The Restaurant at the End of the Universe*). It can get extremely complicated when you try to make logical sense of why things are the way they are. Why are you here? What is the meaning of all this? Why is there so much love and dazzling beauty in one moment and pain and violence in another? Why do you feel the divine's hot breath one night and a cold vacancy the next? Why are there so many wildly different belief systems to choose from? Why did that particular love end or that tragedy occur? Why do families dysfunction or friendships dissolve or personal

EXISTENTIAL *Hiccup*

beliefs get thrown or cute little puppies die or birds get crushed by cars or cute little fishies get all eaten up bye-bye, yum-yum fish sticks? I mean what, really, is the *point*?

Approach spirituality from a purely analytical standpoint, and I can guarantee that you'll come away with a massive migraine with a spicy side of existential angst. It's your choice. Try and tackle these classic, metaphysical brain twisters that philosophers and theologians have been struggling with for centuries and spend your whole life tying yourself up in infinite knots, or accept the mystery, the divine paradox, let go of trying to figure it all out, and enjoy the endless crazy ride.

It's a basic truism of those shimmering down the spiritual path: The more you learn, the more you realize you don't know squat. Admitting that you haven't the slightest clue as to what the hell is really going on might be the ultimate cosmic secret of enlightenment. Sitting on this type of surreal cosmic whoopee cushion often results in sudden moments of divine hilarity and broad perspective, wondrous happenings that keep you on your toes and teach you how to be secure in your *un*knowing. This truism also keeps you open to change, nonjudgmental of others and their diverse experiences, and helps you avoid getting too lazy or convinced or spiritually smug. Having a sense of humor about all this helps you stop taking yourself, your spirituality, and your beliefs so damn seriously. As Oscar Wilde said, "Life is too important to be taken seriously." And as twentieth-century British writer G. K. Chesterton stated, "Angels can fly because they can take themselves lightly" (p. 140).

My friend now understands that her teacher's random outburst happened for all of the preceding reasons as well as the fact that it's been proven through the ages that humor, when it's authentic, positive, and well timed, can often heal an issue faster than the sagest advice. Laughter is one of the quickest ways to instantly crank up not only your vibration but also the vibrations of those around you. It is a most necessary tool for igniting your divine spark.

No Laughter? No Heaven

Martin Luther, the famous German priest and scholar (1483–1546) who initiated the utterly serious Protestant Reformation, said that if there was no laughter in heaven, he didn't want to go. I can't help but agree. Something that has always bothered me in my studies of religion is the astounding *lack* of humor in all those holy texts. (Where are some good puns? Why is everyone so damned serious and dour and *heavy*?) And it's not just the religious texts. A sense of grim humorlessness pervades far too many religious institutions, rituals, and even many alternative spiritualities. As Nietzsche said, "We should call every truth false which was not accompanied by at least one laugh" (*The Portable Nietzsche,* p. 322). This lack of lightness can be a serious problem; it creates a tight, dense energetic space from which lots of holier-than-thou and know-it-all attitudes and even belligerent, violent, cold-hearted behaviors emerge. Too many of us (not to mention entire cultures and societies) link spirituality with moping seriousness. This simply could not be more wrong. I'm here to tell you, the divine has a *wicked* sense of humor (kind of dirty, actually, but let's stay on the laugh track for the moment). Aristotle said, "The gods too are fond of a joke," and he should know. I think. And essayist Agnes Repplier said, "Humor distorts nothing, and only false gods are laughed off their earthly pedestals." Yes, I tend to get a little mistrustful of those spiritual folk who are not willing to tickle the universe's armpits—or let the divine tickle theirs—and have some fun.

I was fortunate to meet the Dalai Lama on my twenty-first birthday. (Don't ask me how it happened on *that* day—sheer luck.) Here's the amazing thing about the Dalai Lama: When you meet him, what strikes you most profoundly about this incredible spiritual master and peacemaker is *not* just his wisdom or the way he radiates calm. No, what told me that I was in the presence of probably one of the holiest people I would ever meet was his intense *humanness*. His ability to totally be himself. Lightly. (I have this one particularly dear memory of him bending down and hoisting up his maroon and yellow monk robes in order to pull up his slouching maroon socks. I just couldn't believe that he was so relaxed and casual in front of guests, and that I actually saw the Dalai Lama's bare calves!)

His Holiness (that's his official title) had just come back from a large conference at which the world's most prominent and well-respected religious leaders had gathered to discuss world peace and the future role of religion in promoting humanitarian aid. The Dalai Lama told us about a particularly serious religious leader who attended the conference who was ultra proper and holy; people were all in awe of him and bowed down to him and opened doors for him, and almost everyone there was very intimidated by his presence. This holy man gave a very solemn and staid speech at the conference, but when he concluded his remarks and moved to

sit down, the large string of prayer beads he was wearing suddenly broke, and hundreds of little beads scattered everywhere, ricocheting off the microphone, the podium, and another attendee's eyeglasses and flying all over the room, causing many to fish them out of their water glasses. Well, every religious leader in the room was quiet and respectful and acted like nothing had happened. But not the Dalai Lama. He thought it was absolutely hilarious (and it was) and immediately cracked up, aloud, laughing and laughing and not trying to hide a thing. In fact, even when he was just telling us this story, he started laughing so hard again that he got tears in his eyes, and we all started laughing with him, and, well, it was the best meeting with a holy person I have ever had. He certainly knew how to spread the light.

Let There Be Gas

One of my favorite stories of divine hilarity happened about ten years ago at the beginning of a Christmas Eve mass (though I'm not Catholic anymore, I still oblige my parents by attending Christmas mass with them once a year, which, by the way, is a gorgeous service, if you ever get the chance), a time when my whole family gets fairly tense due to all the Christmas shopping and meal planning and chaotic airport pickups, and so on. The church was packed, beautifully aglow with the light of hundreds of candles, and piping out very soft and angelic music. All was still and quiet and lovely.

My elder sister was sitting about four people down from me in our pew, and at one point during the service, I desperately wanted to get her attention to tell her something terribly important (like "Oh my

⇒ Laugh Yourself Well ⇐

Besides energetically upping your vibration, you've probably heard that laughter has tremendous healing benefits, too. Doctors tell us that belly laughs actually release endorphins, crank up your sagging heart rate, and purge your system of anxiety. Laughter is like an internal massage for the body.

Norman Cousins (1913–1990) was diagnosed with a terminal illness and given six months to live. He looked back on his life and could see depression, worry, and anger, things he realized had deteriorated his health. It all made him wonder, if such negative emotions could affect him so horribly, what about positive ones? With nothing to lose, he tried a little experiment. He rented a hotel room and rented every comedy movie he could find (yes, that's hundreds). He hired a nurse to read him funny stories. He called his friends and had them share with him anything funny they had said, done, or heard. In short, he filled his life with laughter.

You know how the story ends. Believe it or not, he soon enjoyed a full recovery, and lived a long, full, and very humor-filled life.

God, did you see? Michael so-and-so is here and he has whatshername with him"). So I leaned forward and caught her eye, but as soon as I whispered "Elizabeth . . . ," someone behind me passed gas so loudly that it literally reverberated off the pews, the arched ceilings, and the stained glass.

Well, I totally lost it. I started laughing so hard I could barely contain myself. And so did my sister, who, I later found out, thought the distasteful noise originated from *my* body. We laughed so hard we cried, and my whole family started smiling and laughing, and there was this delightful sparkly feeling that all was good with the world (except maybe in that poor person's bowels). It remains one of my favorite experiences in a church to date, and it most definitely brought out the good cheer so needed during the holidays (holy days) for my family. And now I know that when this type of honest humor pops up during sacred rituals, we have truly been blessed by the presence of the divine.

I bet it's true for you, too; some of the most divinely healing moments in your life happen when you're lost in intense, body-shaking laughter. This is especially true when the laughter emerges during a time of intense seriousness and emotional distress. Even saintly Gandhi once said, "If I had no sense of humor, I would long ago have committed suicide." I can't tell you how many times it has happened that a close friend and I are going though something extremely somber and emotionally dramatic (such as one of us relating a trauma, emotional mudslide, or spiritual crisis), when something, somewhere, shoots up between our conversation—a loud whistle from a neighbor, a dog fighting with a tree, a verbal slipup, a sudden bizarre body movement one of us makes, snot flying out of our noses when we are crying—that makes us just fall apart all over the floor. Our issues might not be solved, but after such a direct infusion of laugh-juice, solving them doesn't seem so dramatic and huge anymore. Our perspective has shifted, and we suddenly realize, hey, life is still going on, snot and all, no matter how stuck or lost we feel, and this is somehow, in those precious moments, amazingly reassuring. Mark Twain said, "The human race has only one really effective weapon, and that's laughter. The moment it arises, all our hardnesses yield, all our irritations and resentments slip away, and a sunny spirit takes place" (*Bite-Sized Twain,* p. 34).

Of course, there is a time and place for seriousness and for humor, but I just want to encourage you to look for humor in the sacred. See the hilarity in the holy. Loosen up. Tickle your beliefs. (They're not meant to be carried around on a luminous silver platter, after all.) And don't be afraid to let your self rip on the cosmos. Being irreverent isn't just for the sake of being witty; it's often a necessity. Humor breaks up energetic clogs. It keeps things running smoothly. It makes the Booming Ha Ha Haw that much louder. And Goddess knows, we can *all* benefit from that.

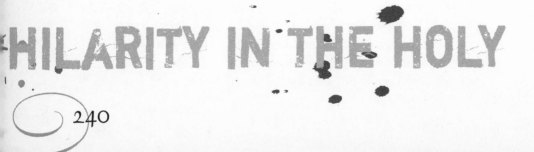

HILARITY IN THE HOLY

CHAPTER 16

Roar

Finale (Like Red Wine
Spilled onto a Mattress)

Let's say you've inflated your soul to the size of a beach ball and it's soaking into the Mystery like wine into a mattress. What have you accomplished? Well, long term, you may have prepared yourself for a successful metamorphosis, an almost inconceivable transformation to be precipitated by your death or by some great worldwide eschatological whoopjamboreehoo. You may have. No one can say for sure. More immediately, by waxing soulful you will have granted yourself the possibility of ecstatic participation in what the ancients considered a divinely animated universe. And on a day-to-day basis, folks, it doesn't get any better than that.

—TOM ROBBINS, *ESQUIRE,* OCT. 1993

You know this is only a beginning. You know this material is far from complete. This book is a match, your life is the kindling. And You are the fire.

Remember, spirituality blossoms your ordinary world, so don't keep it isolated or too far off in the corner. You cannot section off your spirituality from the rest of your life. It has to permeate, saturate, intermix, and get active with all that you are. In other words, God is a *verb,* baby. Igniting your divine spark is nothing less than how you live, and who you are. It is most definitely hands on and hearts open. You must learn to fly while your feet are firmly planted on the ground. Relish the paradox. Celebrate change. Trust your unique process. Igniting your divine spark is one of the most natural, yet brave, things you can do at this time in your life. No less is asked of you now. No less should be expected of you in return.

Realize who you are.

Release your divinity into the world.

We are waiting.

LEARN TO FLY

243

And the day came when the risk to remain tight in a bud was more painful than the risk it took to blossom.

—ANAÏS NIN

JUDGE A BOOK BY WHAT YOU UNCOVER: RESOURCES TO KEEP YOU BLAZING

Contrary to what you might think, the most popular way to explore a given spiritual belief these days isn't via a class or a workshop or by attending a church sermon or even by scouring the all-powerful Internet. It's books. Good old-fashioned ink 'n' paper 'n' glue. In fact, in the next few years, the spirituality category of the publishing biz is set to surpass general fiction in sales; it has hit $2 billion in annual sales and is growing fast. Translation: You've got an incredible array of sources right at your fingertips.

With that in mind, my resource section is like a crazy menu of great mixed cocktails at a really funky bar. There's everything from sixth-century goddess myths from India's Indus Valley to channeled messages from star beings of the 1980s to sex guides and ecstatic poetry and animal spirit symbolism. And they're all invaluable.

247

I can't say it enough: Spirit leaks from every direction, speaks in a variety of voices, and has endless sources. I don't care whether the author is the Dalai Lama or Daffy Duck, when it comes to searching for information that resonates strongly with me, even if it's just the second half of the third sentence in the last paragraph of an otherwise cheesy or dogmatic or throwaway book, I allow myself to learn from it. And so should you. On the other hand, reading anything and everything just because it claims to be spiritual is sort of foolish, too. Remember: resonance. Become a divine filter, a miner of spiritual gold. Pocket the good stuff, and shake out the rest.

Like I said, there are thousands of great books out there; my choices are just the tip of the divine iceberg. There's no rush, no need to go buy 147 new spirituality books and start pounding them down like M&M's. It's a fairly arbitrary selection; your mileage, of course, may vary.

START WITH SOME SPIRITUAL HOT CHOCOLATE
Allegories and parables, metaphors and conspiracy, sex and god, just to get you all cozy and warmed up.

The Alchemist. Paulo Coehlo.
> A simple, elegant literary fable, the classic journey of a shepherd boy in search of riches and wisdom and love and the meaning of life.

The Way of the Peaceful Warrior. Dan Millman.
> An honest, street-level tale of one guy's journey to find his true self by way of an eccentric, chain-smoking mentor named Socrates who works at a gas station. Sort of like *The Karate Kid,* but with better jokes.

Siddhartha. Hermann Hesse.
> The famous slim literary account of one dissatisfied pilgrim
> toward enlightenment. Available in a million used bookstor
> buck or two. Mandatory.

Chasing Rumi. Roger Housden.
> A spare, allegorical tale of one painter's search for the Big Love. Very
> sweet, nicely mystical, and offbeat.

The Tao of Pooh. Jonathan Hoff.
> Perhaps the simplest, loveliest, most charming explanation of the
> ancient Chinese philosophy of the Tao. (Also see the companion
> book *The Te of Piglet.*)

The Celestine Prophecy. James Redfield.
> The New Age classic, surprisingly rich in information about vibration
> and energy and human interconnection, despite the mediocre writ-
> ing. Sort of a fast-paced spiritual adventure tale.

Jitterbug Perfume and *Skinny Legs and All.* Tom Robbins.
> Because it's Tom Robbins. Because he makes the universe swoon
> with his magically delicious metaphors, whacked-out story lines,
> and fiercely horny, divinely human female heroines. *Another Roadside
> Attraction* rocks, too. As does *Even Cowgirls Get the Blues.*

The Da Vinci Code. Dan Brown.
> It's just fun. Tantalizing. That's all I'm saying.

Spirituality for Dummies. Sharon Janis.
> Surprisingly informed, lucid info that's definitely *not* just for dummies.

His Dark Materials: The Golden Compass, The Subtle Knife, and *The Amber
Spyglass.* Phillip Pullman.
> This trilogy paints the most moving, enlightening, heart-opening
> story I have read so far in my life.

ECSTATIC POETRY

Yes, baby, yes. Always a good way to start your day.

Jalaluddin Rumi.

> *The Red Book*'s main man. Look for anything translated by Coleman Barks. This man has done more to help release Rumi's lusciousness to the Western masses than anyone, and all we can say is thank you, thank you, thank you. If *The Essential Rumi* seems a little overwhelming, try *Open Secret* or *Unseen Rain* first; they offer Rumi's simpler quatrains. *The Book of Love* and *We Are Three* should follow. Be sure to read them aloud, too. With wine. Naked. In a bath. And so on.

The Gift: Poems of Hafiz and *Love Poems from God*. Translated by Daniel Ladinsky.

> Hafiz will make you slap your head and giggle like a drunk monkey, and the love poems from a bunch of red mystics will give your spirit all the reminders it needs to wiggle free.

THE GREAT RELIGIONS (HAPPILY, IN CONDENSED, MORE EDIBLE, LESS AUTHORITARIAN FORM)

Try one, try 'em all!

The Essential Kabbalah: The Heart of Jewish Mysticism. Compiled and translated by Daniel C. Matt.

The Essential Mystics: The Soul's Journey into Truth. Edited by Andrew Harvey.

Essential Zen. Edited by Kazuaki Tanahashi and David Schneider.

The Essential Koran. Translated by Thomas Cleary.

The Essential Tibetan Buddhism. Robert A. F. Thurman.

The Essential Jesus: Original Sayings and Earliest Images. John Dominic Crossan.

The Essential Gay Mystics. Edited by Andrew Harvey.

The Essential Tao. Translated by Thomas Cleary.

The Upanishads. Translated and edited by Valerie Roebuck.

The World's Religions: Our Great Wisdom Traditions and *The Religions of Man.* Huston Smith.

Hinduism: A Cultural Perspective. David Kinsley.

The Gnostic Gospels. Elaine Pagels.

Beyond Belief: The Secret Gospel of Thomas. Elaine Pagels.

Prayers of the Cosmos: Meditations on the Aramaic Words of Jesus. Translated and with commentary by Neil Douglas-Klotz.

MYTH, DREAMS, AND THE UNCONSCIOUS: CAMPBELL AND JUNG (WHO ARE PLAYING POKER IN HEAVEN AS YOU READ THIS)

The Power of Myth. Joseph Campbell, with Bill Moyers.

Wonderful explanation of the universal power of myth; perhaps the finest book of its kind. You will never think about *Star Wars* or that classic Nike commercial the same way again. The celebrated PBS DVD featuring a dialogue between Campbell and PBS demigod journalist Bill Moyers is even better. Campbell, one of the great teachers of myth of this century, produced a ton of books; they are all great, although many of them are fairly dense and academic. Start here and venture on.

Man and His Symbols. Carl Jung.

Signs and symbols within your dreams, all spelled out for ya.

Memories, Dreams, and Reflections. Carl Jung.

A memoir, sort of. Definitely a behind-the-scenes glimpse of this great, mystically inclined psychiatrist, with an alchemical, Gnostic twist.

JUNG'S STUDENTS CAN HELP YOU DREAM YOUR SELF AWAKE

The Pregnant Virgin. Marion Woodman.

> Woodman is a Jungian analyst who focuses on the confusion of being, well, us. Female. Young. Sort of messed up in the head. Good stuff.

She: Understanding Feminine Psychology. Robert A. Johnson.

> Because it's good to understand how you're a She and not a He. Also by Robert Johnson: *Owning Your Own Shadow: Understanding the Dark Side of the Psyche.* Helps the reader see that no matter how dark your shit is, it's nothing new and nothing to get too freaked about. And one more: *Inner Work: Using Dreams and Creative Imagination for Personal Growth.* How to learn from dreams when you're wide awake.

Women Who Run with the Wolves. Clarissa Pinkola Estés.

> This is a big book. A bestseller, famous for its re-ignition of the feminine archetype. Don't get overwhelmed by the size; it's chock-full of breathtaking stories, folklore, fairy tales, and dream symbols from all over this planet that still manage speak intimately, to the heart of your unique life.

Goddesses in Every Woman. Jean Shinoda Bolen.

> This book was so inspiring and helpful that by the end of it I was all, "Oh my god, I am SO Aphrodite/Artemis with a pinch of Hera." Diagnose all your friends with a classic goddess archetype and learn how to bring out the best goddess energy in you.

SITTING STILL AND MAYBE NOT TOTALLY SHUTTING UP

Meditation for Dummies. Stephan Bodian and Dean Ornish.

> Yeah, I hate those titles, too. Although we know you're no dummy, this book is an unexpectedly excellent reference for a whole slew of different types of meditation, from Yoga to Zen, visualizations to

AN ORIGINAL YOU

energy work, movement to mantras to dream work and beyond. It even discusses the science of this most ancient of mental calming practices. This is your brain on meditation. Highly recommended.

Meditation for Beginners. Jack Kornfield. Audio CD.
An excellent step-by-step guided practice that stems from Insight meditation, which is similar to Zen. Kornfield's calming voice helps you learn how to work through several different emotions as well as practice important emotional acts like forgiveness, love, peace. Ya know, the big stuff—but in small and simple ways.

Getting in the Gap: Making Conscious Contact with God Through Meditation. Wayne Dyer.
This is a book and audio CD that centers around *japa,* meditation that focuses first on sacred words, then on the space between the words.

Healing Mantras: Using Sound Affirmations for Personal Power, Creativity, and Healing. Thomas Ashley-Farrand.
A slim little book that explains the power of using sound to meditate, be it listening to outside noise or chanting ancient words and prayers. His specialty is Hindu and Buddhist mantras.

The Myth of Freedom and the Way of Meditation. Chögyam Trungpa.
Meditation is not escapism or practiced just to calm your mind or impress your neighbors. It just is what it is, and through practicing it, you should just be who you is. You know? Powerful insights about meditation, from a Tibetan Buddhist perspective.

Creative Visualization Meditations. Shakti Gawain. Audio CD.
Sometimes practicing visualization techniques—you know, imagining things—can help bring us to a state of peace quicker than trying not to think of anything.

Journey into Power: How to Sculpt Your Ideal Body, Free Your True Self, and Transform Your Life with Yoga. Baron Baptiste.

This book is an excellent way to start cultivating a moving meditation practice right in your own living room. Without a lot of the usual fluff, Baron Baptiste offers a fresh, real-world way of getting all calm yet strong with your special self. It's time to get your asana in gear.

Healing Prayers. Ron Roth. Audio CD.

Ron Roth, mystic and healer, guides you through meditative prayer. All you gotta do is sit back and chill out. Although this guy leans towards mystical Christianity and Jesus, he does not necessarily expect you to, and his teachings and methods for prayer and meditation embrace all paths.

Jewish Meditation: A Practical Guide. Aryeh Kaplan.

Learn how to meditate from a rabbi, and learn how meditation has always been interwoven with Judaism.

Wicca: A Guide for the Solitary Practitioner. Scott Cunningham.

This book is a great introduction to Wicca, and it has a helpful section that teaches a few Wiccan meditation practices.

CATEGORY ALL BY ITS VERY OWN SPECIAL SELF

Pronoia Is the Antidote for Paranoia: How the Whole World Is Conspiring to Shower You with Blessings. Rob Brezsny.

Fabulous, crazy, funky wowness. A sumptuous collection of juicy spiritual facts, stories, ideas, and exercises to keep your soul singing celestial show tunes in the cosmic bathroom. A joy, truly, to read. Especially after you've been getting a wee bit too serious about your self and this thing we call spirituality.

SET YOUR INTENTION, DAMMIT!

A New Beginning I: A Handbook for Joyous Survival and *A New Beginning II: A Personal Handbook to Enhance Your Life, Liberty, and Pursuit of Happiness*. Jerry Hicks and Esther Hicks.

OK, these are the classics in New Age intention setting. And the material is, well, channeled. Which means that the lessons and messages were given to Esther Hicks by a group of beings from another dimension called, collectively, Abraham, and she merely wrote them down as they spoke through her. Before you roll your eyes, just try reading some of it on Amazon.com and see whether it speaks to you. If it seems like a little much, try another version of the same information: Lynn Grabhorn's wonderful, down-to-earth book, *Excuse Me Your Life Is Waiting: The Astonishing Power of Feelings*. Or *The Power of Intention* by Wayne Dyer, also an excellent (albeit intentionally repetitive) source for intention setting.

SPEAKING OF GETTING CREATIVE . . .

The Artist's Way: A Spiritual Path to Higher Creativity. Julia Cameron.

All my art-major friends in college would sleep with this inspirational classic under their pillow.

The Creative Habit: Learn It and Use It for Life. Twyla Tharp.

The famed workaholic choreographer maps out her tips and techniques for living a rich, creative life. For Tharp, this means one thing overall: discipline.

Journaling from the Heart. Eldonna Bouton.

Just what the title sounds like.

Creativity and Spirituality. Ram Dass. Audio cassette.

You can find it on Amazon, but the real question is, can you find a cassette player?

255

Succulent Wild Woman: Dancing with Your Wonder-Full Self! SARK.
> I recommend any book by SARK. This groundbreaking, multilayered, handwritten, art-infused, journal-like book will effortlessly inspire you to creatively express all of your yummy, worthy, beautiful true self, and then some. Like the bold and talented author herself, this book demands that you live fiercely, beam brightly, and dance naked in the rain.

SO YOU SAY YOU WANT TO CREATE AN ALTAR . . .
Remember, no pizza boxes . . . unless your prayers like cheese.

Altars: Bringing Sacred Shrines into Your Everyday Life. Denise Linn.

Altars Made Easy: A Complete Guide to Creating Your Own Sacred Space.
> Peg Streep.

A Book of Women's Altars: How to Create Sacred Spaces for Art, Worship, Solace,
> *Celebration.* Nancy Brady Cunningham.

CLASSIC GOODIES OF THE MODERN SPIRITUAL REALM
Time-tested and best-selling cult classics and New Age hits. Some are more dense and challenging than others, but again, just go with what you connect with.

The Power of Now: A Guide to Spiritual Enlightenment. Eckhart Tolle.
> All about how freakin' important it is to stay in the present moment. Tolle does his best to explain this universal truth to us confused, distracted mortals. It's forceful, it's tightly packed, it can be bit of a challenging read, but it's oh so very worth it.

Power Versus Force: The Hidden Determinants of Human Behavior.
David Hawkins.

The beginning of this book sort of turned me off because it was all about how enlightened the author claims he is, which is great and all, but sometimes sounds a bit elitist and intimidating. In fact, the whole "measuring things for their enlightenment quota" put me off at first, but the point behind it, that everything is energy and vibrates at different levels and yes, you can learn to measure it yourself, well, this is something we should all become more aware of in our lives.

The Tao of Physics. Fritjof Capra.

One of the first mainstream books that dared to mix physics with metaphysics and mysticism, or at least show us their similarities. A huge bestseller for its time (the 1970s), now revised and updated. If you love a little deep science with your mysticism, this one's for you.

Cutting Through Spiritual Materialism. Chögyam Trungpa.

Matter-of-factly points out where we often screw up when being all "spiritual." Common distortions and distractions we all can encounter while traipsing down the path.

The Simple Feeling of Being. Ken Wilbur.

A collection of some of this brilliant and prolific philosopher's most moving pieces. This guy is so smart it makes your eyebrows dance. Luckily, he is so plugged in that your heart will boogie as well.

A Path with Heart. Jack Kornfield.

A hugely popular book that was incredibly helpful for me, simply because it clarifies so many aspects of how to remain true to yourself as you journey forth. It has a Buddhist slant, and it reads a little slow and quiet, but speaks to the essence of any spiritual path.

The Places That Scare You: A Guide to Fearlessness in Difficult Times.
Pema Chödrön.
Tools and ideas to help you transform your freaky stuff (anxieties,
fears, stresses) into purring pussycats. The author, a western Buddhist
nun, is nothing short of remarkable.

Wherever You Go, There You Are: Mindfulness Meditation in Everyday Life.
Jon Kabat-Zinn.
Stay present. Stay here. Hey, come back. . . .

The Art of Happiness: A Handbook for Living. The Dalai Lama and Howard C.
Cutler.
How to be truly happy, not fake squinty happy, from the most joyful
human I have ever met.

Thinking Like the Universe: The Sufi Path of Awakening. Pir Vilayat Inayat Khan.
Because thinking like the divine helps you know your self as the
divine. Another one of my faves.

Anatomy of the Spirit: The Seven Stages of Power and Healing. Caroline Myss.
I first listened to the audio CD of this book on a lo-o-o-ng car ride
over a decade ago. It rocked my world. Myss was one of the first to
bring the ideas of spiritual energetics and health to the mainstream.
Her *Invisible Acts of Power* shows just how important it is to do the
little things in life. Any of Caroline's books or CDs are fabulous.
(Aside: If you can, it's always great to listen to the original authors
speak their own stuff. Especially Myss, who has a wit and humor
and a no-bullshit Chicago attitude that drives the material home.)

Conversations with God, Books 1, 2, and 3, and *What God Wants.*
Neale Donald Walsch.
Wonderful, lucid books. Honest. Freeing. Funny. Profound. Not
faith-based or religious per se. Spiritual. Poignant. You know, just

Neale and God sitting down for a little friendly banter, a banter we should all start participating in.

Return to Love. Marianne Williamson.

This material stems from the epic book *A Course in Miracles* (a really, really dense yet profound read). In *Return to Love,* Williamson parses this complicated material and makes it much more modern and funny and applicable to your life.

The Teachings of Don Juan: A Yaqui Way of Knowledge. Carlos Castaneda.

Jungles, spiritual tests, multidimensional visions, and wise shamanic teachings from one of the world's most fascinating shamans. What's not to like?

The Way of the Shaman. Michael Harner.

This guy is a scholar and a shaman and is considered by many to be the MacDaddy of all things shamanistic.

How to Know God. Deepak Chopra.

Chopra explains seven levels of God. He mixes science with meta-physics with spirituality, and he's Deepak, for Pete's sake, so you know he's got the goods.

The Invitation and *The Dance: Moving to the Rhythms of Your True Self* and *The Call: Finding Out Why You Are Here.* Oriah Mountain Dreamer. Check out that name. Have you read her poem "The Invitation"? It filled e-mail in-boxes years ago; everyone and their sister printed it out to use for their future wedding vows. All of her books stem from her gorgeous poems mixed with her personal reflections and inspiring, homegrown wisdom.

Loving What Is: Four Questions That Can Change Your Life. Byron Katie.

All about peeling your onion, and then some. Discusses the importance of questioning the authority of your own beliefs.

STOP HIDING
259

Katie supposedly got enlightened by watching a bug crawl across the floor. Gives us all hope. (Unless you're insectophobic.)

Be Here Now. Ram Dass.

Classic goodie from the 1960s with some serious psychedelic flare. Ram Dass is a very powerful and wise spiritual teacher who at that time was tripping on acid, took off to India, and hung around a profound spiritual master for some time and then came home to set himself and others free.

You Can Heal Your Life. Louise Hay.

Yes, you can. Physical, emotional, spiritual, and mental health can all be helped and healed by, well, you. You have more power than you might realize. Read this, and you'll never look at a pimple or a headache or a cold as *just* a pimple or a headache or a cold. There are hundreds of books about spiritual healing out there, but this is a great introduction.

Your Body Believes Every Word You Say: The Language of the Body/Mind Connection. Barbara Hoberman Levine.

Watch what you say to yourself, because your body is taking notes.

The Four Agreements: A Practical Guide to Personal Freedom (A Toltec Wisdom Book). Don Miguel Ruiz.

Wisdom and cosmography from the Toltec, written simply, eloquently, and in such a way that you can agree to living your whole life better.

The Seat of the Soul. Gary Zukav.

Not the most entertaining read, but informative as hell and a great book to help you start waking up to your metaphysical universe.

Simple Abundance: A Daybook of Comfort and Joy. Sarah Ban Breathnach.

Say "thank you." Make the world better. Simple. Easy. Profound.

Breathnach suggests keeping a gratitude journal in which you write down five things you are grateful for every day—hey, Oprah does it.

The Healing Path of Prayer: A Modern Mystic's Guide to Spiritual Power. Ron Roth with Peter Occhiogrosso.

Ron Roth is a very powerful, well-respected modern-day healer and mystic from my former 'hood, Chicago. Although he leans toward Jesus in his own life, he certainly doesn't push the J-man on anyone else. He's all about connecting you to You. To God. To the universe. To Krishna. To Goddess. Through prayer.

Do You Need a Guru? Understanding the Student-Teacher Relationship in an Era of False Prophets. Mariana Caplan.

An intriguing book that discusses the importance and dangers of hooking up with a guru or spiritual teacher. Caplan does, in fact, have a guru herself. She's a professor, and she eloquently argues for having a teacher on your path. In fact, she goes so far as to claim that no one can really "make it," spiritually speaking, without surrendering to a teacher. Now, anything that says "only" makes me say "baloney," but then again, I could be saying that 'cause I'm all ego-ish and individualistically western and have not surrendered to a teacher. In any case, this book is a provocative and extremely helpful read, and I highly recommend it to anyone considering working with a spiritual teacher.

SHE-SHE POWER! RIGHT ON! KICK ASS! GO TEAM, GO!
Wicca and Mary and goddesses and the divine feminine. Bring it *on!*

The Spiral Dance: A Rebirth of the Ancient Religion of the Goddess. Starhawk.

Pagan/Wiccan wisdom from one of the most beloved witches of all. Mother Earth needs us, ladies. Now.

What does your spirit whisper!

Drawing Down the Moon: Witches, Druids, Goddess Worshippers, and Other Pagans in America Today. Margot Adler.
Great research into modern pagan life.

A Witch Alone: Thirteen Moons to Master Natural Magic. Marian Green.
Like Scott Cunningham's *Wicca,* a great introduction to Wicca. Very earth-friendly, goddess lovely, and empowering. These books help you experience the power of Wicca on your own.

Hindu Goddesses: Visions of the Divine Feminine in the Hindu Religious Tradition. David Kinsley.
A wonderful taste of the goddess in India.

Encountering the Goddess: A Translation of The Devi-Mahatmya and a Study of Its Interpretation. Thomas B. Coburn.
This ancient myth from India is about the Goddess kicking some major demon ass!

Kali: The Feminine Force. Ajit Mookerjee.
There are some amazing, sometimes downright freaky images of the intense goddess Kali in this one.

The Woman's Encyclopedia of Myth and Secrets and *The Woman's Dictionary of Signs and Symbols.* Barbara G. Walker.
Finally, a feminist encyclopedia and dictionary! So when you have a crazy dream or step on a snail, you will know what it might mean for your sexy *female* self, instead of his. Plus, these books have some funky trivia that will wow your friends at dinner parties.

The Gospel of Mary Magdalene. Translated by Jean-Yves Leloup.
Told from Mary's point of view. Supposedly. The male apostles really couldn't deal with the fact that Mary was BFF with JC. Read all about it. Cryptically.

262

Tantra: Cult of the Feminine. André Van Lysebeth.
> Sort of dense and subjective but also deeply informative portrayal of Tantra.

Note: The following five books stem from a time (1970s to early 1980s) when a great many archaeological studies were being conducted on the divine feminine in ancient cultures. Digging up ancient goddess icons and artifacts had two effects on the women who found and studied them: They became both incredibly excited and extremely angry at the patriarchal forces that apparently had swept into these ancient cultures and stomped all over what these women believed were peaceful, goddess-loving, pro-female societies. Today, a good deal of this scholarship has been disproved (the cultures might not have been as utopian as some had hoped), but the exciting and positive energy and power that ignited these amazing female authors and researchers is something we should all welcome into our lives. After all, the truth of needing a resurgence of the divine feminine energy *is* truth.

The Myth of the Goddess: Evolution of an Image. Anne Baring and Jules Cashford.

When God Was a Woman. Merlin Stone.

The Chalice and the Blade: Our History, Our Future. Riane Eisler.

The Great Cosmic Mother: Rediscovering the Religion of the Earth. Monica Sjöö.

The Living Goddesses or just about any book by pioneering archaeologist Marija Gimbutas.

The Woman Awake: Feminine Wisdom for Spiritual Life. Regina Sara Ryan.
> An electric glimpse of twenty-four powerful and unique female spiritual teachers from several different traditions and paths. The divine feminine shows up in a variety of forms. Take note. Look around your corners.

Longing for Darkness and *The Bond Between Women: A Journey to Fierce Compassion.* China Galland.

> Beautifully written, honest books that combine Galland's passionate research of the divine feminine (the Buddhist Tara, the Hindu Kali, the Catholic Black Madonna) with her personal stories and insightful, heartfelt reflections.

A Woman's Journey to God: Finding the Feminine Path. Joan Borysenko.

> Wonderful and empowering read about one woman's search for and embrace of her distinct path amid a sea of more male-based spiritual ideas, teachers, and traditions.

Enduring Grace: Living Portraits of Seven Women Mystics. Carol Lee Flinders.

> An up-close and stirring view of female Christian mystics. Some of them seriously rocked the house. Some of them just prayed for its support. But they still kicked some spiritual ass.

At the Root of This Longing: Reconciling a Spiritual Hunger and a Feminist Thirst. Carol Lee Flinders.

> Feminism for the spirit. Eastern and Western wisdom is woven into the author's illuminating personal story. What's at the root of your longing?

LET'S FUNK IT UP A BIT, K?

Weirder, more esoteric, more provocative, but no less inspiring works for the fringe mystic in you.

Numerology and the Divine Triangle. Faith Javane and Dusty Bunker.

> Figure out the meaning behind your name and birthdate and his name and birthdate. Did you know the universe speaks in numbers?

Animal-Speak: The Spiritual and Magical Powers of Creatures Great and Small and *Nature-Speak: Signs, Omens and Messages in Nature.* Ted Andrews. These books give the meanings behind all the animals and plants growing through your world. Nature is talking; are you listening?

The Hidden Messages in Water. Masaru Emoto.
The water guy from the movie *What the Bleep Do We Know!?* Emoto now has a bunch of books out, and they all discuss the same thing: how our thoughts, intentions, words, and prayers affect the shape and intricate formation of water crystals (and, by extension, the human body, which is 50 to 70 percent water). And he has the stunning, ultra-close-up photographs to prove it.

Seth Speaks: The Eternal Validity of the Soul. Jane Roberts.
More channeled material from a spirit being called Seth. Heavy stuff. Sort of complicated, but deeply profound. I guarantee that this book is on most spiritual teacher's bookshelves, whether they believe in channeling or not.

The Sense of Being Stared At: And Other Aspects of the Extended Mind. Rupert Sheldrake.
An open-minded yet discerning scientist who studies the paranormal, Sheldrake helps explain why your dog knows she's going to the vet way before she *should* know. Also psychic parrots. And how you can sometimes sense who's calling *before* you pick up the phone, and other cool stuff like that.

Why God Won't Go Away: Brain Science and the Biology of Belief. Andrew Newberg, Eugene d'Aquili, and Vince Rause.
Scientists study how we are, quite literally, wired for God. Yes, even you. Even if you call God *you.*

The Psychic Pathway: A Workbook for Reawakening the Voice of Your Soul, and, *Trust Your Vibes: Secret Tools for Six-Sensory Living.* Sonia Choquette.
In a realistic, funny, and grounded way, Sonia Choquette teaches you how to develop your psychic abilities, raise your antennae, and trust your senses. All of 'em.

Second Sight and *Positive Energy: 10 Extraordinary Prescriptions for Transforming Fatigue, Stress, and Fear into Vibrance, Strength, and Love.* Judith Orloff.
A psychic psychiatrist who is another great teacher of energy work, psychic information, and how to connect with your inner healer.

Many Lives, Many Masters: The True Story of a Prominent Psychiatrist, His Young Patient, and the Past-Life Therapy That Changed Both Their Lives.
Brian L. Weiss.
This is the book I read in sixth grade that made my priest faint. Documents reincarnation, spirit guides, the afterlife, and other dimensional goodies.

What the Bleep Do We Know!? Film on DVD.
This cult hit is a favorite in indie theaters around the nation. Rent the DVD. Watch it. Watch it three times. Admire Marlee Matlin's surreal performance, and never look at reality—or basketballs, or weddings—the same way again. Hilarious animations. Metaphysics and quantum physics and funny genius philosophers. Check out the books based on the movie as well.

The Matrix. Film on DVD.
As cliché as it's become, *The Matrix* is still a great one to dissect, meta-physically speaking. And it doesn't hurt that Neo is, of course, hot. Plus, those black latex outfits and uber-cool shades bring out the sexy fierce goth angel in us all.

SKEWING A WEE BIT YOUNGER

Spilling Open. Sabrina Ward Harrison.

Sabrina Ward Harrison created this masterpiece when she was just a tiny young thing (like, about sixteen) and now has several artistically awesome, super-creative feminine angst and joy books based on her personal journals. You will never journal the same after perusing Harrison's books.

What Would Buffy Do? The Vampire Slayer as Spiritual Guide. Jana Riess.

It's Buffy. She's campy and quirky and fights like a fiend. Slaying demons and vampires is just part of her job. As is wearing cute outfits. As is spitting out profound and hilarious bits of wisdom. And figuring out her place in the world. Joss Whedon, I love you. Go rent some of the shows on DVD, and sigh.

Becoming a Goddess of Inner Poise: Spirituality for the Bridget Jones in All of Us. Donna Freitas.

Love Bridget Jones? Hate Bridget Jones? This is still a fun, informative, empowering book. And the author has great shoes.

Dharma Punx. Noah Levine.

A young man's story of punk rock, drugs, and rage and how Buddhism helped him transform his rebellion through a healthier medium. He still punks out. He still rages. But now he does it while being conscious. And nonviolent. Cool.

Blue Jean Buddha: Voices of Young Buddhists. Edited by Sumi D. Loundon.

Wonderful collection of personal anecdotes and experiences from young peeps just like you, who share how aspects of Buddhism have greatly enriched and transformed their life. Not typical. Not smarmy. Not preachy. Just real.

Killing the Buddha: A Heretic's Bible. Edited by Peter Manseau and Jeff Sharlet.
Generation Us writers and thinkers waxing and moaning and celebrating and questioning and being all super-smart about spirituality.
And Haven Kimmel's chapter, "Revelation," is written from the
allusive perspective of angelic beings, and it is quite possibly one
of the coolest and smartest pieces of its kind I've ever read. Ever.

Daily Afflictions: The Agony of Being Connected to Everything in the Universe.
Andrew Boyd.
Wise, twisted, sardonic, and so very needed. Paradox is how you learn
to live bigger. When things suck and get darker than dark, stay conscious. Please. Or you might miss an amazing opportunity.

Sexy Witch. LaSara FireFox.
Sexuality and spirituality and bad-ass witchy wisdom for the modern
young alternative gal who's all about empowering her self, becoming
more sexually truthful and bold, performing some downright beautiful rituals, and creating a life that's more her own. Witches have some
seriously great sex. Seriously.

SPEAKING OF SEX . . .
Because connecting to your sexual energy in a real and honest and
juicy way is one of the most divine things you can do.

Transcendent Sex: When Lovemaking Opens the Veil. Jenny Wade.
Yes, you too can touch the divine via sex without practicing at all.
Just check out all her case studies. This book proves that sex is an
often overlooked but no less important and viable tool for rubbing
noses with the universe.

The Soul of Sex: Cultivating Life as an Act of Love. Thomas Moore.
All about infusing sexual energy into *all* of life, not just during the

268

EVERYTHING IS

act itself. The sexual energy Moore explores is less Cosmo and more Red. It's the authentic spirit of sexuality, not the media's caricature.

For Yourself: The Fulfillment of Female Sexuality. Lonnie Barbach.
Great sex info based on clinical research and women's groups. Orgasm info, emotional issues, relationship communication, the importance of masturbation. Very helpful for us all.

Healing Love Through the Tao: Cultivating Female Sexual Energy. Mantak Chia and Maneewan Chia.
Intriguing info about sexual energy and orgasms. This book is quite serious about sex as a spiritual practice. Not a lot of room for vibrators. Good thing you won't take it *quite* that seriously.

Tantra: The Art of Conscious Loving. Charles Muir and Caroline Muir.
This couple was one of the first to westernize Tantric sex and hold successful workshops in Maui. A little cheesy, definitely touchy-feely, but the point—to deepen your connection to your self, your partner, the divine—is all good. And hey, waking up your G-spot is always a fun thing to do on a lazy Sunday morning.

The Art of Sexual Ecstasy. Margot Anand.
Another popular sacred sex teacher along the lines of the Muirs, but a little less cheesy.

Any book by educator and sexpert Violet Blue.
Honest and funny and very, very dirty, she is very pro-woman, pro-healthy, pro-real, honest sex. Raw and up-front, and she seriously cares. Highly recommended.

Bootyparlor.com
Wonderfully girly and friendly and super-sassy site that celebs frequent. Try the Bathtime Kit.

Goodvibrations.com
> The original ultra-friendly, easygoing, sex-positive, female-owned and female-run sex shop. Super-educational yet still fun and ground-breaking.

Babeland.com
> A little more daring than goodvibes, but no less friendly and helpful. Also female-owned and female-operated.

Tinynibbles.com
> Sex educator and author Violet Blue's personal site. Info on all her books is here, too.

AND NOW, ON TO THE NET

Of course, you know that many of the authors listed above have wonderful Web sites of their own, right? Following are a few more to add to your Spiritual bookmarks.

killingthebuddha.com
> Smart and meaningful Web site dedicated to our spiritually jaded generation.

freewillastrology.com
> Rob Brezsny's fantastic site, which is oh so much more than just astrology. Join his newsletter for the most profoundly hilarious and informative astrology columns, like, ever. (He also wrote *Pronoia Is the Antidote for Paranoia,* which I listed earlier in its own category.)

spiralmuse.com
> Women. Art. Social activism. Spirituality. Healing. Good stuff.

imagesofdivinity.org
> Wonderful resource for pictures and information about the divine feminine.

pluralism.org

> Another amazing resource for checking out many sorts of religions and alternative practices in your area or across the country.

academicinfo.net/religindex.html

> Site that leads you to all sorts of other sites about all sorts of spiritual and religious stuff.

Beliefnet.com

> The classic catch-all Web site for all types of religion and spirituality. If they don't have it here, it might not exist.

gnosis.org

> Tremendous site with great articles and other info about Gnosticism.

lipstickmystic.com

> Funky, girly site with a lot of cool 'n' playful spiritual and energetic info (and some strangely funny cat pictures that I still haven't quite figured out). Created by a sassy, intelligent woman who's a writer, a psychic, and an astrologer all wrapped up in one.

AUDIO

If you want to hear any of the spiritual teachers I've listed talk their walk, check out these fabulous audio companies for DVDs and CDs, cassettes and MP3 downloads.

nightingale.com

soundstrue.com

audible.com

SELECT BIBLIOGRAPHY

Adams, D. *The Restaurant at the End of the Universe.* (Reprint ed.) New York: Del Rey, 1995.

Ahmed, L. *Women and Gender in Islam: Historical Roots of a Modern Debate.* New Haven, Conn.: Yale University Press, 1993.

Allen, Mary. "Spirit Versus Ego" http://thinkholistic.com/newspub/story.cfm?id=256

Alexander, A. *The Secrets of Jin-Shei.* San Francisco: HarperSanFrancisco, 2004.

Andrews, T. *Animal-Speak: The Spiritual and Magical Powers of Creatures Great and Small.* St. Paul, Minn.: Llewellyn, 2003.

Andrews, T. *Nature-Speak: Signs, Omens, Messages in Nature.* Jackson, Tenn.: Dragonhawk, 2004.

Bach, R. *Illusions: The Adventures of a Reluctant Messiah.* (Reissue ed.) New York: Dell, 1989.

Barbach, L. *For Yourself: The Fulfillment of Female Sexuality.* New York: Signet, 1976.

Benson, H. *The Relaxation Response.* New York: Avon Books, 1976.

Bernadin, T. "Metros Versus Retros: Are Marketers Missing Real Men?" Speech by CEO of Leo Burnett Worldwide, Cannes, France. [http://www.leoburnett.com/news/press_releases/2005/prjun22-91722.asp]. June 22, 2005.

Bixler-Thomas, G. "Understanding Dreams: Perspectives from the Ancients Through Modern Times." [www.ondreaming.com/theories]. Nov 1998.

Bo, K. B. "Sexuality as a Locus of Spirituality." [www.rcrc.org/resources/publications/sexspirituality.htm]. n.d.

Breathnach, S. B. *Simple Abundance: A Daybook of Comfort and Joy.* New York: Warner Books, 1995.

Brezsny, R. *Pronoia Is the Antidote for Paranoia: How the Whole World Is Conspiring to Shower You with Blessings.* Berkeley: Frog, 2005.

Brown, D. *The Da Vinci Code.* New York: Doubleday, 2003.

Campbell, J., with Moyers, B. *The Power of Myth.* (B. S. Flowers, ed.). New York: Doubleday, 1988.

Capra, F. *The Tao of Physics.* (4th ed.) Boulder, Colo.: Shambhala, 2000.

Castaneda, C. *The Teachings of Don Juan: A Yaqui Way of Knowledge.* New York: Washington Square Press, 1985.

Chesterton, G. K. *Orthodoxy.* Vancouver, Canada: Regent, 2004.

Chia, M., and Chia, M. *Healing Love Through the Tao: Cultivating Female Sexual Energy.* Huntington, N.Y.: Healing Tao Books, 1986.

Cousins, N. *Anatomy of an Illness as Perceived by the Patient.* New York: Norton, 1979.

Cummings, E. E. "A Poet's Advice." In *A Miscellany Revised.* (G. J. Firmage, ed.). New York: October House, 1965.

De Mille, A. *Martha: The Life and Work of Martha Graham.* New York: Random House, 1991.

Doniger, W. *Dreams, Illusions, and Other Realities.* Chicago: University of Chicago Press, 1984.

Douglas-Klotz, N. *Prayers of the Cosmos: Meditations on the Aramaic Words of Jesus.* San Francisco: HarperSanFrancisco, 1990.

Eck, D. L. *Darsan*. New York: Columbia University Press, 1998.

Eliade, M. *Patterns in Comparative Religion*. (R. Sheed, trans.). Lincoln: University of Nebraska Press, 1996.

Ellington, S., and Green, M. C. (eds.). *Religion and Sexuality in Cross-Cultural Perspective*. New York: Routledge, 2002.

Emoto, M. *The Hidden Messages in Water*. Hillsborough, Oreg.: Beyond Words, 2004.

Enuma Elish, Vol. 1: *The Seven Tablets of Creation;* Vol. 2: *The Babylonian and Assyrian Legends Concerning the Creation of the World and of Mankind.* (L. W. King, ed.). London: Booktree, 1998.

Feuerstein, G. *Tantra: A Path of Ecstasy*. Boston: Shambhala, 1998.

Feuerstein, G. *Sacred Sexuality: The Erotic Spirit in the World's Great Traditions*. Rochester, Vt.: Inner Traditions, 2003.

FireFox, L. *Sexy Witch*. St. Paul, Minn.: Llewellyn, 2005.

Francoeur, R. (ed.). *The International Encyclopedia of Sexuality*. New York: Continuum, 1997.

Freud, S. *The Ego and the Id: The Standard Edition of the Complete Psychological Works of Sigmund Freud*. (J. Riviere, trans.; J. Strachey, ed.). New York: Norton, 1962.

Freud, S. *The Interpretation of Dreams*. (A. A. Brill, trans.). New York: Avon, 1980.

Furst, P. T. *Flesh of the Gods: The Ritual Use of Hallucinogens*. New York: Praeger, 1992.

Gandhi, M. *The Essential Gandhi: An Anthology of His Writings on His Life, Work, and Ideas*. (L. Fischer, ed.). New York: Vintage, 2002.

Graff, D. E. *Tracks into Psychic Wilderness: An Exploration of Remote Viewing, ESP, Precognitive Dreaming, and Synchronicity*. Boston: Element Books, 1998.

Harper, K. A. *The Roots of Tantra*. Albany: State University of New York Press, 2002.

Hawkins, D. R. *Power Versus Force: The Hidden Determinants of Human Behavior*. Carlsbad, Calif.: Hay House, 1985.

Hoeller, S. A. "A Gnostic Worldview: A Brief Summary of Gnosticism." [http://www.webcom.com/~gnosis/gnintro.htm]. n.d.

Hooker, R. "Early Christianity: The Early European Church." [http://www.wsu.edu:8080/~dee/CHRIST/EUROPE.HTM]. 1996.

Javane, F., and Bunker, D. *Numerology and the Divine Triangle*. Atglen, Penn.: Whitford Press, 1979.

Johnson, R. A. *Inner Work: Using Dreams and Creative Imagination for Personal Growth*. San Francisco: HarperSanFrancisco, 1989.

Johnson, R. A. *She: Understanding Feminine Psychology*. San Francisco: HarperCollins, 1989.

Johnson, R. A. *Owning Your Own Shadow: Understanding the Dark Side of the Psyche*. San Francisco: HarperSanFrancisco, 1993.

Jung, C. G. *Man and His Symbols*. New York: Dell, 1968.

Jung, C. G. *Synchronicity*. (R.F.C. Hull, trans.). Princeton, N.J.: Princeton University Press, 1973.

Jung, C. G. *The Archetypes and the Collective Unconscious*. (G. Adler, ed., and R.F.C. Hull, trans.). New York: Bollinger, 1981.

Jung, C. G. *Memories, Dreams, and Reflections*. (A. Jaffe, ed.; C. Winston and R. Winston, trans.). New York: Vintage, 1989.

Jung, C. G. *The Undiscovered Self*. (R.F.C. Hull, trans.). Princeton, N.J.: Bollinger, 1990.

Kabat-Zinn, J. *Wherever You Go, There You Are*. New York: Hyperion, 1995.

COSMIC DUTY

King, K. L. *The Gospel of Mary of Magdala: Jesus and the First Woman Apostle.* Santa Rosa, Calif.: Polebridge Press, 2003.

Kinsley, D. R. *Hinduism: A Cultural Perspective.* Upper Saddle River, N.J.: Prentice Hall, 1993.

Kornfield, J. *A Path with Heart: A Guide Through the Perils and Promises of Spiritual Life.* New York: Bantam Books, 1993.

Kripal, J. J. *Kali's Child: The Mystical and the Erotic in the Life and Teachings of Ramakrishna.* Chicago: University of Chicago Press, 1998.

Kripal, J. J. *Roads of Excess Palaces of Wisdom: Eroticism and Reflexivity in the Study of Mysticism.* Chicago: University of Chicago Press, 2001.

Kripal, J. J. *The Serpent's Gift: Gnostic Reflections on the Study of Religion.* Chicago: University of Chicago Press, 2006.

Krishnamurti, J. *The Meditative Mind.* Ojai, Calif.: Krishnamurti Publications of America, 1989.

Lawrence, D. H. *The Letters of D. H. Lawrence,* Vol. 1: *September 1901–May 1913.* Cambridge, England: Cambridge University Press, 1979.

Levine, B. H. *Your Body Believes Every Word You Say: The Language of the Body/Mind Connection.* Fairfield, Conn.: Wordswork Press, 2000.

Levine, N. *Dharma Punx.* San Francisco: HarperSanFrancisco, 2004.

Lysebeth, A. Van. *Tantra: The Cult of the Feminine.* York Beach, Maine: Weiser, 2002.

Manning, S. T. *Psychology, Symbolism, and the Sacred: Confronting Religious Dysfunction in a Changing World.* Otsego, Mich.: PageFree, 2004.

Matt, D. C. (comp. and trans.). *The Essential Kabbalah.* San Franciso: Harper-SanFrancisco, 1996.

McIlroy, A. "Hard-Wired for God." *Globe and Mail* (Toronto), Dec. 6, 2003, p. F1.

Mookerjee, A. *Kali: The Feminine Force.* New York: Destiny Books, 1998.

Myss, C. *Anatomy of the Spirit: The Seven Stages of Power and Healing.* New York: Three Rivers Press, 1997.

Myss, C. *Invisible Acts of Power: The Divine Energy of a Giving Heart.* New York: Free Press, 2004.

Newberg, A., d'Aquili, E., and Rause, V. *Why God Won't Go Away: Brain Science and the Biology of Belief.* New York: Ballantine Books, 2002.

Nietzsche, F. "Thus Spoke Zarathustra: A Book for Everyone and No One." In W. Kaufmann, ed. and trans., *The Portable Nietzsche.* New York: Penguin, 1959.

Nietzsche, F. *The Gay Science.* (B. Williams, ed.; J. Nauckhoff trans.). Cambridge, England: Cambridge University Press, 2001.

Owens, L. S. "An Introduction to Gnosticism and the Nag Hammadi Library" [http://www.gnosis.org/naghamm/nhlintro.html]. n.d.

Pagels, E. *The Gnostic Gospels.* New York: Vintage, 1989.

Pagels, E. *Beyond Belief: The Secret Gospel of Thomas.* New York: Random House, 2003.

Patton, K. *A Magic Still Dwells: Comparative Religion in the Postmodern Age.* Berkeley: University of California Press, 2000.

Phillips, R. B. *Representing Woman: Sande Masquerades of the Mende of Sierra Leone.* Los Angeles: UCLA Fowler Museum of Cultural History, 1995.

Pick, D., and Roper, L. *Dreams and History.* London: Routledge, 2003.

Radin, D. *The Conscious Universe: The Scientific Truth of Psychic Phenomena.* San Francisco: HarperSanFrancisco, 1987.

Repplier, A. *Points of View.* Boston: Houghton Mifflin, 1891.

Robbins, T. "You Gotta Have Soul." *Esquire,* Oct. 1993, p. 164.

Roebuck, V. (trans. and ed.). *The Upanishads.* (rev. ed.) Chicago: Penguin, 2003.

Roth, R., with Occhiogrosso, P. *The Healing Path of Prayer: A Modern Mystic's Guide to Spiritual Power.* New York: Three Rivers Press, 1998.

Rumi, J. *The Essential Rumi.* (C. Barks with J. Moyne, A. J. Arberry, R. Nicholson, trans.). San Francisco: HarperSanFrancisco, 1995.

Rumi, J. *The Mathnawí of Jalálu'ddín Rúmí.* (ed. R. A. Nicholson, with critical notes, translation, and commentary), Vol. IV, Book 3. London: Gibb Memorial New Series IV, 1930.

Satyananda, S. *Kundalini Tantra.* (2nd ed.) Munder, Bihar, India: Bihar School of Yoga, 1996.

Schimmel, A. *Mystical Dimensions of Islam.* Chapel Hill: University of North Carolina Press, 1975.

Sheldrake, R. *The Sense of Being Stared At: And Other Aspects of the Extended Mind.* New York: Crown Publishers, 2003.

Smith, H. *The World's Religions: Our Great Wisdom Traditions.* San Francisco: HarperSanFrancisco, 1991.

Tanakh: The Holy Scriptures, The New JPS Translation According to the Traditional Hebrew Text. Philadelphia: Jewish Publication Society of America, 1985.

Tolle, E. *The Power of Now: A Guide to Spiritual Enlightenment.* Novato, Calif.: New World Library, 1999.

Turner, V. *The Ritual Process: Structure and Anti-Structure.* New York: Aldine de Gruyter, 1995.

Twain, M. *Bite-Size Twain: Wit and Wisdom from the Literary Legend.* New York: St. Martin's Press, 1998.

Twain, M. *The Wit and Wisdom of Mark Twain: A Book of Quotations.* Mineola, N.Y.: Dover, 1999.

Urban, H. B. *Tantra: Sex, Secrecy, Politics, and Power in the Study of Religions.* Berkeley: University of California Press, 2003.

Vatsyayana. *The Essential Kamasutra.* (W. Doniger, trans.) Audio CD. Louisville, Colo.: Sounds True, 2003.

Wade, J. *Transcendent Sex: When Lovemaking Opens the Veil.* New York: Paraview Pocket Books, 2004.

Wiesner, M. E. *Christianity and Sexuality in the Early Modern World: Regulating Desire, Reforming Practice.* London: Routledge, 2000.

Weiss, B. L. *Many Lives, Many Masters: The True Story of a Prominent Psychiatrist, His Young Patient, and the Past-Life Therapy That Changed Both Their Lives.* New York: Simon & Schuster, 1988.

White, D. G. (ed.). *Tantra in Practice.* Princeton, N.J.: Princeton University Press, 2000.

Whitman, W. *Leaves of Grass: His Original Edition.* New York: Viking Press, 1959.

Williamson, M. *Lectures Based on a Course in Miracles.* Audio program. Chicago: Nightingale-Conant, n.d.

IMAGINATION

ACKNOWLEDGMENTS

I am grateful to so many people for helping me with this project:

First and foremost, to my parents, Bill and Tater: two of the most open-minded, nonjudgmental, uniquely spiritual role models a modern young woman could ask for. Your incredible generosity, your heartfelt pride in all three of your wacky daughters, your eloquent and profound guidance, and your wonderful sense of humor have helped me more than words can say. Here are just a few: Thank you. Thank you. And thank you.

To Mark: my partner in spiritual crime, *The Red Book*'s personal fire starter, my love. You have well exceeded your duties as a significant other and will be honored in the celestial Boyfriend Hall of Fame, eternally surrounded by callipygian fire goddesses who will serve you delectable full-course (scorch-free) dinners while massaging your feet with Scharffen Berger chocolate and Bonny Doon Framboise. You helped conceive this book and have been its (ahem, très manly) womb, providing nonstop support; physical, mental, and spiritual nourishment; amazingly positive encouragement; a wicked sense of humor; and belovedly honest advice. Thank you for being the ultimate sounding board, the ever-patient brilliant and witty editor, the main reason I have not gone totally insane, and the only reason *The Red Book* is readable. Merci, gracias, thank you.

To my sisters (flesh and blood), Caroline and Elizabeth: two of the most radiant, intuitive, and creative women I know. Elizabeth: Your loving gift of the original red book began it all. Caroline: Your ongoing and awesome "I'm gonna dress you for *Oprah*" support has kept me fueled. To you both: Without your infinite patience, your always eerily wise advice, your twisted Beak humor, well, my life would totally be at a loss and this book would lack its heart. And I wouldn't eat nearly as many organic vegetables or wear such fabulous designer jeans. Thank you.

To my other sisters (extended family and cosmic): Megg(li), my lady: Without you, red would just be a color. With you, I AM more. My thanks stretches lifetimes, universes, car rides. You have given wings to my heart and watered my soul and laughed with me till the big fat dirty angel peed himself. Our purple retirement home awaits. . . . Rachel: wise prophetess embedded within a bubbling beauty. I don't know how I would have made it this far without your effervescent spirit always nudging me further and providing noodles and the most patient ears ever. I have treasured your unconditional love and support throughout my life.

And to the rest of my ladies, whose oh-so-red lives have deeply inspired this book and whose hearts have always opened mine: Simmin, Allison, Kubie, Tor, Dana, you are all so remarkable, and because you have all touched me so, your energy and spirit infuses every page of this book. Also Nicole, my sassy sista from Tucson, who, despite our never having met in person, has helped me beyond what I can say here: Your heart, your cosmic wisdom, your raw humor, your extraordinary insight I am so deeply grateful for. To the Red Ladies:

Priya, Jenny, Sharon, I am grateful for our giddy, open-ended talks and sacred pregnant pauses. Thank you all for the poignant advice, the sensitive ears, the total witnessing. To my lovely coworkers at UCSF—Sarah, Heather, Mary Anne, Deborah, and all the wonderful people at the School of Pharmacy: Your graciousness and support and flexibility have allowed me to support myself while I pursue my dreams. Thank you all so much.

To my family (flesh and blood): Grandmother Beak, the brilliant grand matriarch of us all who inspires my life like no other, and Grandfather, who is chuckling at us all from heaven. Paul Schmidt, Nancy and Richard, Amy, Craig, Kristin, Susan. Uncle Jimmy, Marcy, cuzzin David, Tracy. The Peelers: Granddad and Barbara, Uncle Lee and Aunt Nancy, Lee and Madeleine, Theresa, Christine, Grace, Ray and Susie. Cecy and wonderful writer and personal inspiration Chris, and Nolan and Nick. Also Henry and, of course, last but never least, the fast-talking, big-hearted spiritual warrior herself, Gaily Wailey.

To my family (extended and cosmic): The Grays: Beth, Jim, Carter, Allison (my cross-country soulmate), and Alex, who helped me grow up with lots of love and copious amounts of easy laughter. The Barrecas: Fay, Steve, Chris, and young Steve, whose heartfelt compassion and down-home irreverence have made my life so much richer and funnier. "The Wolves": all the amazing moms a girl could dream of. The Conants: Marilee and Vic, for all your help and wonderfully inspiring e-mails. Each and every one of the Roberson clan. To Seth, for your endless support and unbounded creative energy and long, calming phone calls; Oliver, for your twinkling spirit and artistic genius with designing the headline font for the cover of this very book; Jay, for making me oh so grateful for the power of true friendship; Dana, Nicholas, and Janai, for your compassion, guidance, humor, and help

283

on so many levels. Finally, to Megan Scott, Lynette Daubt, Susan March, Sandy Fawcett, for your healing touch and care.

To my teachers: Professor Kepes of Woodlands Academy, who encouraged me to read Jung when I was sixteen, allowing me to open so many closed doors. Professor Joel Smith of Skidmore College, my mentor, my friend, the one who allowed my dreams to come bursting into the classroom, who allowed the goddess to come bursting from my heart, who always challenged me to go further. Professor Schweder of the University of Chicago, who sat next to my family in that Miami airport. By connecting me with Calcutta, you changed my life. Hena Basu, whose wisdom and gentle care made Calcutta feel like home. Professor Kimberley Patton of Harvard, who brought heart and compassion and kindness to the classroom, who encouraged me to speak up and out, who revealed the magic within the academic study of religion and encouraged me to feed the magic that dwells inside me. Finally, Professor Jeffrey Kripal, who made my final year at Harvard one of the most sacred and powerful experiences of my life. You dared me to transform lines into circles, to dance the between, to be my self. You allowed and inspired the first red paper, which then led me straight to this book. Thank you.

To my wonderful editor, Julianna Gustafson, who fought so enthusiastically for this book to exist: Your angelic eyes, devilish sense of humor, and warm heart dance throughout this book. I am forever grateful to have someone as kind and supportive and "tapped in" as you for my first editor. Thank you for your patience, for your delicious mystical wisdom, and for sending me those adorable pictures of your dog on a day when I really needed to see adorable pictures of a dog (and especially because her name is Buffy). Every author should be this blessed. Also to Catherine Craddock, Andrea Flint, Sandy Siegle,

Carolyn Uno, and Paula Goldstein, for your kind and creative suggestions and nonstop giddy support. And to all the rest of the many wonderful people at Jossey-Bass and Wiley, thank you all so much.

To my agent, Anna Ghosh, who had the guts to take on an inexperienced, first-time spirituality writer who had never written a complete chapter: Thank you for your patience, unflinching support, and hard work; you have been a joy to work with. Paul Morris, for your generous help, and Dan Strutzel, for going beyond the call of duty. Neale Donald Walsch, SARK, Baron Baptiste, Rob Brezsny, LaSara FireFox, China Galland, Cameron Tuttle—thank you so much for your support and enthusiasm and willingness to spread the Red. You have all inspired me greatly.

And of course, to the Wiggling Wow, the Divine She, Aya, Ofolo, Anaya the Gurgling Grey, Red, and all the other beings and spirits and winged things and chocolate that have supported my silly ass for eons: Thank you.

THE AUTHOR

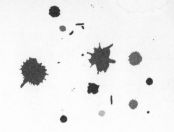

This is Sera Beak's first book—in this life. She may write another. Or she may just stop trying to explain the inexplicable and build a bird sanctuary. Or she might finally create that cool toy for young girls she's been dreaming about. She is happiest being a mover. But not of furniture. She lives in San Francisco, drives a purple car, cohabits with an effusive African Grey parrot named Anaya, and has an unnatural affection for human bloopers. She would love to hear from you. And You.

www.serabeak.com